DISCOVER

LOGOSYNTHESIS®

The Power of Words in Healing and Development

DR. WILLEM LAMMERS

——— THE ORIGIN OF ———
LOGOSYNTHESIS®

Logosynthesis® is a registered trademark of Dr. Willem Lammers.
You may not use it without the express consent of the author.

This book contains excerpts from Willem Lammers' book
*Self-Coaching with Logosynthesis: How the Power of Words Can
Change Your Life* (2015) and *Logosynthesis. Healing with Words:
A Handbook for the Helping Professions with a Preface by Dr. Fred
Gallo* (2015), which have, however, been substantially completed,
updated, and completely reworked for this edition. The names and
personal data of the clients in this book have been changed.

If this publication contains links to third party websites, we assume
no responsibility for their content, as we do not adopt them as
our own, but merely refer to their status at the time of the first
publication.

—

Copyright ©2020, Dr. Willem Lammers, The Origin of Logosynthesis®

Bristol House, Bahnhofstrasse 38, 7310 Bad Ragaz, Switzerland.

www.logosynthesis.net, info@logosynthesis.net

First edition 2020, version 26.09.2020.

ISBN 979-8671078268

Translated from German by Emmanuella Uka,
edited by Raya Williams and Willem Lammers.

Cover design Max Kolpak, typesetting Tharanga Gamage.

PLEASE READ THE DISCLAIMER ON P. 167!

CONTENTS

ADVANCE PRAISE

Logosynthesis has become a discreet and indispensable part of my life, like a real fascination. It's simple, and yet precise formulations have freed me from many daily inconveniences and the energetic stickiness. However, in these carefully chosen words, there is not only the power to consciously free myself from small things, but also the potential to transform, perhaps even redeem, deeper and more frightening things. Thank you for this versatile and rewarding process.

– Ariadne von Schirach, philosopher, bestselling author, and university lecturer

This little book offers a brief overview of what Logosynthesis is and how it is applied. It is a guide for immediate self-application and an introduction for professionals in the field.
Willem Lammers has managed to succinctly summarize the development of Logosynthesis, the basic attitude, and the Basic Procedure. The examples presented illustrate how Logosynthesis works. The steps are clearly described and easy to understand, whether you are hearing about Logosynthesis for the first time or are already familiar with its practice.

Willem's field model brings new aspects to the change, growth, and development of human beings in nature and culture. It appears at the right time as we are becoming aware again of how we depend on one another. Logosynthesis gives new impulses for the development of your life in the world.

— Dr. med. Suzanne von Blumenthal, psychiatrist, psychotherapist, head of the Institute for Logosynthesis®
Bad Ragaz, Switzerland

I am grateful to Willem with all my heart for his work and his gift to humanity—because that is precisely what it is. In my 14 years of top-class sport, I have always looked for ways to overcome obstacles and resistances on the way to my goals, to live my true greatness. Willem's work, Logosynthesis, is a central building block on my way to Olympic victory and to my expertise in successfully achieving spectacular goals! Logosynthesis, my constant companion: simple, unconventional—ingenious!

– Tanja Frieden
Olympic champion, energy coach

The time has come to live your life filled with meaning and joy, despite your circums-tances and perceptions of reality. Discover

Logosynthesis teaches you the basics of how to remove blocks that get in the way of your peacefulness, creativity and talent. You'll use words to move energy, previously bound in frozen structures of beliefs, fantasies and memories. You can then enhance your life's mission by uniting the best of your innate essence with the current path of your physical life. Choices and options become clearer, as well as the means to achieve them. Give yourself the gift of freedom by discovering Logosynthesis.

— Lori Chortkoff Hops, Ph.D., DCEP
Licensed Psychologist, Reiki Master
President-elect 2020-Association for
Comprehensive Energy Psychology
Westlake Village, California USA

It is the task of psychotherapy to relieve and heal suffering. Willem Lammers shows convincingly, compactly and readable, how this is done with Logosynthesis—through "the power of words." In my opinion, Logosynthesis impresses for several reasons: The human being comes into view as a whole; body, emotions and thoughts together are of central importance. The person can become capable of control and action again, as the energy starts flowing and "I take it back to the right place in my Self." Transparent basic assumptions, clear interventions, concrete instructions and encouraging case vignettes—I read the book and benefitted greatly. I am sure that you will feel the same way while reading it!

– Prof. Dr. Helga Kohler-Spiegel,
university professor, psychotherapist,
teaching supervisor, book author

SANDRA PLAYS THE PIANO

Sandra is under stress when she has to play the piano. She says:

I watch myself play the piano, and I get all tense.

She says the first sentence of the Logosynthesis sequence:

I retrieve all my energy,
bound up in the image of me playing the piano,
and I take it to the right place in my Self.

Her reaction:

I feel some relief.

She receives and repeats the second sentence:

I remove all non-me energy
related to this image of me playing the piano
from all of my cells, all of my body and
my personal space,
and I send it to where it truly belongs.

Her reaction:

I feel sad and I can't play anymore.

She receives the third sentence:

I retrieve all my energy,
bound up in all my reactions to this image of me
playing the piano,
and I take it to the right place in my Self.

She gets very quiet, then she says:

I'm playing music, not notes!

FOREWORD

"Should" has a limit.

"Can" has none.

– BYUNG-CHUL HAN

I'm glad this little book has reached you. It contains an up-to-date introduction to the Logosynthesis model and its most important method, the Basic Procedure. Logosynthesis is a revolutionary system to help people heal, grow, and develop. It helps you to examine, understand, and resolve blocks— whether they be physical, emotional, or in your thoughts. The working principle to achieve this is unusual: the power of words.

Once you engage in Logosynthesis, over time, it will become a valuable companion in meeting the challenges of your daily life. Its procedures become a daily routine, like meditation, yoga, or prayer. This practice helps you to recognize your life goals and focus on them.

If you want to know more after reading this book, you'll find more information about the world of Logosynthesis in the appendix.

This book was written, translated, and edited with the help of many people. I am grateful for this support, especially from Luzia, my long-time partner, without whom Logosynthesis, in its present form, would hardly exist. Emmanuella Uka translated the manuscript from German, Raya Williams edited it, Max Kolpak designed the cover, and Tharanga Gamage did the typesetting. Also, my Logosynthesis colleagues Pamela Burkhalter and Shanda Woodin gave the finishing touch to the English edition.

Finally, I would like to thank all those who accompany me daily in the development and dissemination of Logosynthesis, their support has been invaluable at every stage of this project.

Bad Ragaz, September 2020,

Part I.

THE FRAMEWORK OF LOGOSYNTHESIS

It's the framework that changes
with each new technology and not just
the picture within the frame.

– MARSHALL MCLUHAN

As a human being in the world, you are continually evolving. However, your evolution can be inhibited, interrupted, or come to a complete stop. A sudden shock, a loss, an accident or trauma, or even some unfriendly words—all these events and many others may disturb, inhibit, or block your development.

Logosynthesis can help you to resolve such blocks and continue your life path in the service of your mission. Logosynthesis is based on a coherent and fascinating energy concept that goes beyond psychology and biology. The model does not only consider the body and mind as energy phenomena: it also includes the source of energy, your Essence. Your environment has its place in the model as well: It consists of a set of socio-energetic fields within a larger whole—the Matrix.

5

Within the Matrix, you can apply the methods of Logosynthesis to various areas: to your family, your friendships, your love relationships, workplace, finances, daily habits, and spiritual practices. Logosynthesis can restore the flow of your life energy and help you to live and love at your highest potential.

Part I of this book describes the origin, the development, and the world model of Logosynthesis. If you prefer to work with the methods immediately, you can skip part I and II and come back to it later. In this case, go to Part III and start with the "Who's in the chair?" exercise on page 65.

1.

THE BEGINNING: NEXT TO HER SHOES

After this there is no turning back.

– MORPHEUS

It all started on January 11, 2005. On that day I had an appointment with a 45-year-old woman, Leonore. She was suffering from a range of physical and psychological symptoms. Following a mysterious fall in a train station six years before, she could no longer concentrate. She had to give up her job and had never been the same since. Doctors had found no neurological damage and even thought she was making it up.

Leonore was deeply troubled by these events and could no longer find her way in life. She had no memory of what had happened early that morning. A few hours after the fall, she had regained consciousness—in an unknown place, injured and with damaged clothing. All she remembered was that she had tried to get on a train, but she hadn't been able to open the doors.

The morning before our appointment, something similar had happened in the bathroom: She wanted to open the shower cubicle but her hand couldn't find the doorknob. It wasn't the first time, and she said, discouraged: "I'm next to my shoes." In her Swiss dialect this expression means that someone is crazy.

Leonore looked at me with big, hopeful eyes and asked me if I thought she was crazy, too. I didn't feel that way. Her body and her mind were in two different places in the room—even though that may sound improbable.

To her right, I saw a thin, light shadow, like a veil or a mist. Normally, I would have dismissed such a perception as fatigue or as a fantasy on my part, but her words resounded loud and clear in my ears:

"I'm next to my shoes."

Was she actually next to her shoes, not as a metaphor, but literally? Had she put a part of herself in another place when she fell?

I shared my observation with Leonore and asked her if she could put these two pieces together—her body sitting in the chair and the misty shadow to her right. She reacted timidly at first but succeeded on the second attempt. To my astonishment and hers, intense emotions arose, and suddenly she became aware of what happened on that fateful morning at the railway station.

Through her tears, she was able to tell me exactly what had happened: She had been overrun by a hasty passer-by and had fallen down the stairs onto the cold concrete. When she was finally able to get up, she had been very confused and had lost all orientation. She had wandered around for hours until she finally managed to call her husband to come and pick her up.

Leonore was extremely relieved that she had recovered her memories and finally knew what had happened. The division in two parts in space was gone.

The experience impressed me deeply and I began to investigate the laws behind this event. I knew from my experience as a psychotherapist that people's consciousness can be split in different parts. What was new to me, however, was that such parts are actually in different places in space and can be alive in their own way. One part of Leonore was the physical body, and the other part was trying to control the muscles of that body.

Since then, I gradually discovered that the space around us is populated with virtual images and voices. We react to these as if they were really there.

That was the start of what became Logosynthesis®[1] as a comprehensive model for alleviating human suffering and stimulating personal growth.

My first session with Leonore confirmed that consciousness can exist separately from the physical body in space and time. With this knowledge, I was able to understand that such a split prevented normal functioning: Leonore had been unable to think and concentrate properly, she had been unable to control her physical coordination—the flow of her life energy was interrupted, and her mind and body were not communicating properly. This discovery was followed by many more similar ones.

In the following session, Leonore described panic and fear of an upcoming appointment with an insurance doctor. The doctor was to assess her ability to work. A few months earlier, she had had a violent argument with another doctor, who had yelled at her, accusing her of making up symptoms. As she was telling me this, she moved her head to the right, as if this doctor was still in the room, screaming in her left ear.

I followed my intuition again and asked Leonore if she could remove the disturbing image of the doctor from the room. With a little encouragement, she succeeded. To her astonishment—and

---

[1] Logosynthesis is a registered trademark of Dr. Willem Lammers.

10

mine—the fear of the next appointment with his colleague melted away in the same moment.

In each of these examples, I had invited Leonore to visualize a memory—with the purpose of making it less threatening with the help of an imagery technique. I discovered, later, that the power of words can facilitate this process: You can neutralize painful memories, fantasies and beliefs by saying simple sentences.

From these experiences, a new model for healing and development was born: Logosynthesis. The name tells it all: In ancient Greek, *logos* stand for meaning, spirit, word, or teaching. *Synthesis* means bringing together or merging. Logosynthesis means "bringing together with words." Literally.

The model and its methods help you to understand and change the human energy system. Once you have become familiar with the principles, Logosynthesis is efficient, effective and easy to apply. Many elements of the model are not new and may already be familiar to you. I have combined psychological and philosophical concepts from many schools with timeless spiritual knowledge. The result of this development is surprising again and again—even for me after years of experience with the model.

You can use Logosynthesis in many areas: Whether it's to relieve everyday anger, sadness, guilt, and shame, to resolve deeply traumatic memories, a threating fantasy, or a limiting belief. This book offers an introduction to Logosynthesis as a guide and support for self-help and personal development. If you want to know more, have a look at the resource section at the end of the book. If you're a professional in coaching, counseling, psychotherapy, or education, you can follow a path of training and certification to use the model in your practice.

Let us begin with how we see the human being from the perspective of Logosynthesis.

2.

THE HUMAN BEING
IN LOGOSYNTHESIS

There is a space between stimulus and reaction.
In this space, we have the freedom and power, to choose our
reaction.
In our reaction lies our growth and our freedom.

– VIKTOR FRANKL

In this chapter, I'll introduce the way we think about human beings in Logosynthesis. It is no coincidence that its name reminds of Viktor Frankl's logotherapy. His model was one of the first to expand psychotherapy to include the spiritual dimension.

We are all beings in search of meaning. We are biological, psychological and spiritual beings—body, mind and spirit. In everyday life, these three aspects of our existence are hardly separable. The distinction is helpful when we want to examine our life as a whole or when a single area seems problematic. Let us now explore each dimension in more detail:

1. We are a *physical body* with the needs of the material world. With the help of our senses, we pick up and react to information from the outside world. Our body is designed for survival and has corresponding needs. It must eat, drink, avoid danger and reproduce. For this, it needs energy. The underlying science of biology, therefore, examines the processes of life and survival in what I like to call the *Earth Life System*.

2. We also exist as a *mind*. We adapt to the environment, we cope with rain and drought, heat and cold. We make clothes and build houses; we modify our original environment and create a new one. We set personal and collective goals and do our best to achieve them. We create procedures, rules, and values, that help us in knowing how to behave. The mind knows the world and its obligations, limits and possibilities. It is capable of learning and can deal with people and tasks. The mind also has needs: To feel safe and to develop, we need attention, contact, security, stability and variety. Psychology is the science that examines our ability to actively shape life in the context of our environment and our relationships.

3. The third dimension of our existence is the spiritual. We are more than body and mind. We are *Essence*, beings beyond space and time, who grow and develop continuously. We actively shape our world from inspiration and creative

intent. Essence gives meaning to our lives. It examines the truth of our existence. It is this spiritual dimension that gives Logosynthesis a deeper meaning and explains its effectiveness: Essence manifests you as a human being on this earth with a mission and with the potential to fulfil that mission. I have consciously chosen the neutral term "Essence" so that you can translate and integrate it into your world view. The spiritual dimension is part of the human experience in every culture. You will recognize elements of familiar spiritual traditions in the Logosynthesis model—Judeo-Christian, Taoist, Buddhist or Islamic. You can start from any frame of reference and experience and approach the Logosynthesis model with an open mind. It's designed to include every single person on the planet.

Learning and practicing Logosynthesis will increase your awareness of Essence. From there you can overcome challenges and blocks in meaningful areas in your life:

- lifestyle and future plans
- decision making
- artistic intuition
- scientific inspiration
- relationships
- personal values
- religion and mysticism

In the worldview of Logosynthesis, the first cause of suffering in the world is the loss of awareness of your Essence. Restoring this connection allows your life energy to flow freely, with an enormous potential for healing, presence, creation and manifestation which keeps unfolding.

3.

ESSENCE AND THE SELF

We are luminous beings,
not this coarse matter.

– MASTER YODA

You enter this world of space and time as a manifestation of Essence: A Self. Your Self comes with a unique personal mission and also with the potential to fulfill this mission in this lifetime. Your body and your mind are the instruments of this Self; they enable you to live on earth. Many people tend to believe that they *are* their body or their mind—They identify with the needs, sensations, emotions, and thoughts of their bodies and minds.

They are deeply convinced that there is nothing more. The materialist worldview of our society, dominated by physics, chemistry, biology and psychology, strengthens such a belief system. These people have lost contact with Essence, the real and only reason for their existence. Logosynthesis supports people in their reconnection to Essence, thus enabling a recall and a return to a deeper meaning—a person's mission in life.

Disturbances in the flow lead to suffering

When you're learning Logosynthesis, you start from the assumption that your life energy is either flowing or it is bound, stored in energy structures. The free access to the source of your life energy can be interrupted, blocked or restricted for various reasons. Then life loses its meaning and you suffer.

A higher Self, an immortal soul, a divine being beyond space and time has been part of human experience for thousands of years. However, in the current western world view, this experience is pushed into the background. I assume that every form of human life begins with an intention from our Essence.

Your existence in this world is accompanied by a meaning, a mission, a task. You are in this world for a reason. You're not a biological machine with a humid computer between your ears. You are here to investigate, to learn, to do, to serve, to create, to lead, to follow or simply to be: Every life has a purpose, including yours.

Essence—your immortal Soul, the divine You, your Source—creates your Self from its inexhaustible life energy.

Essence builds a body with billions of cells and countless functions, a hardware for your Self. This body enables you to explore the world in space and time, to move around in it, and to absorb and transmit information.

Your Essence also creates a mind to process information. The mind is like the software on your computer. It helps you design your life and carry out your plans. Your body and mind are tools for your mission, your task in this existence. However, you are not your body or your mind, even if you think so, or even if it feels that way.

There is an incredibly complex process going on when your Essence manifests as a Self with an intention, when you enter this world as a human being with a body and with a mind. If this transition succeeds, all of a person's life energy is available for their task, but there are many obstacles on your path into the world.

Sometimes, the journey is finished already before birth or shortly after, and we don't know why. If you are reading this book, you have found your way into the world. Now it is all about removing blocks and freeing up your energy where it has become frozen: That's the way you will be able to find and engage in your mission.

4.

THE SELF IN
THE MATRIX

**The subject does not belong to the world;
rather, it is a limit of the world.**

– LUDWIG WITTGENSTEIN

Your Essence chooses this world in space and time as a learning environment for a new Self—for you as an individual human being. Through your conception and birth, you enter this environment that I call *the Matrix*. You probably know this term from the movie trilogy of Lana and Lilly Wachowski. In the movie, the Matrix is a gigantic, collective energy field with many possibilities and merciless boundaries. Even gravity is subject to the Matrix.

In our Logosynthesis terminology to describe reality, the Matrix is such a field. It dictates the codes, rules, and values for families, groups, organizations, tribes, cultures, nations, and the world. *Socio-energetic fields* in the Matrix determine your place in society—where you live, what you learn, what you do and with whom. The most important of these fields are gender, class, and ethnicity. These extremely strong fields determine key parts of your identity in the Matrix.

However, you are more than a cog in the great machine of the Matrix: You are Essence, and that's what makes your life interesting. Although you are in the Matrix, you do not belong to it: You are *in* the world, but not *of* the world. Your Self, the interface of your Essence and the Matrix, makes you unique, different from any other human being.

When you enter the world, the energy of your Essence meets the energy of the Matrix and its fields. This is a tremendous challenge, even a shock. Why?

- You come from an environment where there is neither space nor time.
- Birth, the entry into the three-dimensional world is connected with high physical distress.
- Your body has hunger and thirst; it may be too cold or too warm.
- Your mind does not know the world and must learn how it works.
- Parents and society define your body and mind.

There are two extremes in this transition process:

1. The material pole.
   Through the physically challenging transition, the consciousness of your higher nature fades. The Matrix almost becomes the only

reality you can perceive. The characteristics of your body and mind are defined and determined by the Matrix, and it binds your energy for its own continued existence. The Matrix uses the energy of individuals to create, shape and maintain its contents, functions, and structures. In return, it provides predictability. At this extreme, life has no further meaning than staying alive. Many people notice that they are missing something when the needs of their bodies and minds are fulfilled. This often happens after the first half of life.

2. The immaterial pole.

At this extreme, you ignore the Matrix. Your consciousness is primarily determined by Essence and your mission. If this is the case, sooner or later you will notice that something is restricting the free flow of your energy. You experience the world as if it is disturbing, inhibiting, or blocking who you really are. You know what you are here for, but you do not recognize what is in your way. Because you do not really perceive the Matrix, you cannot use its potential and resources in the service of your mission.

Most people move between these two extremes. They are aware that their lives have meaning. They no longer see the forest of Essence for the trees of the Matrix. Every human being has a life task and must find their form: A unique, personal balance between the two aspects of existence. This also applies to you, to your Self.

All patterns in perceptions, emotions, thoughts, values, beliefs, and behavior appear and develop in the field of your Self, at the interface of your Essence and the Matrix. This field distinguishes you from all other people. It is, therefore, worthwhile to examine it more closely: It is yours!

How to find your way

The following questions will help you to solve many life problems. Your answers will help you to set priorities, make decisions, avoid disturbances, and plan your future. You will reflect on your qualities and get support and help from the Matrix. Without answers to these questions, the old wisdom of Michel de Montaigne applies:

If you don't know where you're sailing to, every wind is a headwind.

The questions are:

- *What is your life task in this world?*
- *Why did you choose this environment, this corner of the Matrix, for this mission?*
- *When, how and where do you experience the Matrix as disturbing your path?*
- *When, how and where do you experience the Matrix as supporting your path?*

Part II.

ENERGY IN LOGOSYNTHESIS

*Perhaps life energy does not exist at all,
but in spite of our ability to be definite about this subject,
there are so many things which happen as if there were such a
force, that it is easier to understand human beings if we
suppose that life energy does exist.*

– ERIC BERNE

Logosynthesis is based on the principle that everything in the universe is energy. All other aspects of the model and its methods are derived from this assumption. This leads to three further principles, which are stated in a simplified form here:

– *Energy is either frozen or it is in flow.*
– *Energy either belongs to you or doesn't.*
– *Words move energy.*

Together, these assumptions form the framework for the theory and methods of Logosynthesis; they also explain its effects. At this moment, there is no scientific proof of the existence of the phenomena and mechanisms described in this book—yet. You can consider them as working concepts in the way physicists assume the existence of a particle before it is officially discovered. In the meantime, let the above assumptions explain your daily experience in practice and the astonishing accounts of significant change resulting from their applications. The lack of empirical validation need not keep you from experimenting with the methods of Logosynthesis. Thousands of people have experienced the power of words first-hand.

If you're skeptical, I invite you to consider the energy model in this chapter as a metaphor. Whenever something new appears in the world, people try to explain it with the help of metaphors, allegories or parables. They enable us to understand something new in terms of what's familiar. Here are three examples:

-   When the deeper processes of the mind were still unknown, Sigmund Freud explained them using the physics of the steam engine. The unconscious thus became a "cauldron of seething excitement."
-   Current cognitive psychology often compares the human mind to a computer with input, output, and an operating system.
-   Jesus Christ said in a parable that those who translate His teachings into deeds are like a man who builds his house on solid rock. When a flood of water came, it could not harm the house because of its solid foundation.

Metaphors and stories make it possible to understand an unknown environment when we don't have all the facts. In the case of Logosynthesis, the energy metaphor helps to answer the key question in any form of healing and development: How to live a life of meaning and joy?

I like the above-quoted statement by Eric Berne, the master of transactional analysis. Let's assume that life energy exists and see what becomes possible. This part of the book discusses the effect of this force in Logosynthesis.

5.

WHAT IS ENERGY?

> If you want to find the secrets of the universe,
> think in terms of energy, frequency and vibration.
>
> – NIKOLA TESLA

You probably use the word energy regularly without thinking about its meaning. In Logosynthesis, the term is indispensable for making complex processes comprehensible. In this chapter, I would like to give you an understanding of energy.

Physical energy

Physics has many, but no clear definitions for the term energy. In everyday language, energy is the possibility to make a difference:

- motion: driving a car
- heat: boiling water
- power: switching on the computer
- fire: lighting the fireplace

From the perspective of physics, energy can flow freely, like when you step on the gas or turn up the heating. Energy can also be stored, as fossil fuel, in a battery or in a reservoir in the Alps. Seen from biology, plants, animals, and humans need energy to live. They receive this energy from sunlight or food.

Subtle energy

In Logosynthesis the term *energy* has a broader meaning. We assume that everything that exists is energy, and that it has a certain frequency or vibration. Matter has the lowest vibration, followed by energy in the physical sense, as described above. Information and consciousness have higher frequencies. The highest frequency has the intention or power to create or manifest something. It is associated with a power that's higher than we can grasp or understand with our conscious minds. Your Self is a manifestation of this power, but its field is infinitely stronger.

Many ancient cultures know the concept of life energy. This is a subtle form of energy that makes life possible. This life energy has different names like Qi in Chinese, Prana in India and Physis in ancient Greece. In Logosynthesis we call it Essence. Your Essence creates an energy system through an intention. This appears in the form of a living body and a mind with an identity. Only Essence makes your life possible and gives it meaning.

Many biologists and psychologists are skeptical about the concept of life energy, or they refuse to take it into consideration.

Sigmund Freud rejected the idea of a creative force:

Religion is an illusion and it derives its strength from the fact that it falls in with our instinctual desires.

Rudolf Virchow said in 1860:

Medical science [...] has proven that life is only the expression of a sum of phenomena, each of which follows the known physical laws.

Max Planck, the physicist, had a different opinion:

All matter originates and exists only by virtue of a force which brings the particle of an atom to vibration and holds this most minute solar system of the atom together.
We must assume behind this force the existence of a conscious and intelligent mind. This mind is the matrix of all matter.

Biologist Rupert Sheldrake describes our bodies as:

...nested hierarchies of vibrational frequencies that occur as discrete systems within larger systems and more complicated. A world of vibrational structures from those basic to the increasingly large and increasingly complex.

According to Sheldrake, the body is embedded in a larger whole:

> *In fact, the entire universe, from subatomic particles to more complex life forms, nebulae and galaxies, can be regarded as a huge set of energy resonance fields, all of which are in constant interaction with each other.*

Sheldrake, therefore, assumes that the outside world can influence the body:

> *Therefore, it is quite plausible to believe that externally imposed vibration can have an influence on our physiology.*

Sheldrake's assumptions can be translated one-to-one into the Logosynthesis model.

Disturbances in the System

When the free flow of energy in your system is interrupted or blocked, the conscious awareness of your Essence disappears into the background, and you lose sight of the meaning and purpose of your life. As a result, you are less able to recognize opportunities and to avoid dangers. You won't treat others well, you'll make a mountain out of a molehill, or you become fearful or aggressive at the wrong moment. You notice that your reactions are more suited to a child than to an adult. When energy cannot and does not flow for a longer period, equal relationships with other people are only possible to a limited extent. If this lasts even longer, you can become ill.

Two key features

In the frame of reference of this introductory book, the energy concept of Logosynthesis has two key characteristics:

1. *Energy either flows freely—or it is frozen. Logosynthesis helps to release blocked energy and to bring it into motion.*
2. *Energy either belongs to you—or it doesn't. Through Logosynthesis you can move energy to where it really belongs.*

If your energy is in flow, it is available for your mission; it's not split off in rigid structures and not bound outside of your field. Now we will examine these key properties in more detail.

If we look at it more closely, we can see that the energy flow is not simply on or off. In fact, it vibrates at different frequencies. However, for the purpose of an introduction to the field, it's best to start with a simplified version of the model.

6.

ENERGY FLOWS FREELY—OR IT IS FROZEN

**Flow with whatever is happening
and let your mind be free.**

– ZHUANG ZHOU

This chapter deals with the first key characteristic of our concept of energy:

Energy either flows freely—or it is frozen.

Energy in flow

Your life energy behaves like waves or like particles. Waves are in flow: They move freely in a quantum field outside space and time. Particles, on the other hand, are rigid and bound in space and time. When you live in contact with your Essence, your energy flows freely and is available for your mission, your life task. You perceive the presence of the Matrix and can react appropriately to the opportunities and challenges in your environment. You recognize blocks and can dissolve them, avoid them, overcome them or come to terms with them. You can also recognize opportunities in the Matrix and use them as steppingstones to move forward on your life path. In a permanent learning process, your mission becomes clearer and clearer.

Your life is a dance, but dancing needs to be learned and practiced. You have to learn what is useful for your mission and fulfilling the tasks that belong to it. There are classic roles, such as father, mother, bus driver, production worker or secretary. Some people take on other forms of responsibility. They take on leadership, do research, heal people, write books, make art, or entertain people on stage or in a stadium.

Every human being has their own task for his existence at this moment with these people in this place. If you are aware of this, you engage with it of your own accord and dedicate yourself to your life task, your mission. Sometimes, the conscious access to this knowledge is blocked or veiled—then the meaning of your life is elusive.

In an ideal life, all your energy is in flow and is in harmony with your tasks, mission and goal. You are a whole that is part of a larger whole—like a cell in an organ or like an organ in a body. You know about your task and you stick to it. You are connected to higher, wider consciousness and you know it. Once you have understood why you are in this world, you navigate and decide consistently in terms of, and in line with, your mission.

This is the ideal situation. Reality is more prosaic for most of us. Only part of your life energy vibrates at such a high frequency. Other parts vibrate at lower ones or have been brought to a complete standstill. That is life, and I'm no exception. A long series of challenging events in my own life have led me to develop Logosynthesis, with the purpose of restoring the flow of frozen energy.

Energy structures

To orient yourself in three dimensions in time, you need a dynamic balance between flowing and bound energy. If too much of your life energy is flowing, the supporting structure will be missing. It will be difficult for you to concentrate, and you are easily overwhelmed. If too much of your energy is bound in rigid patterns, you cannot react nor act meaningfully.

Energy structures support or limit. Supporting structures offer a frame of reference that help us to function in daily life on earth. They act like lighthouses in a sea of impressions and events in everyday life. Limiting structures, on the other hand, cause problems. They do not offer orientation but lead to inappropriate or inadequate reactions: too much, too fast, too little, too late. People and events along our life path can influence this balance. They can bind your life energy or create a space in which you can free it.

How does energy freeze?

Before a new human being sees the light of day, their energy is in flow and in contact with their Essence. They have no place in the world yet. Also, they have not yet learned to know their body and mind, including their needs. Needs are complex, and realistically, can only be partially fulfilled and met— even by the most ideal caregivers—and that is painful. The baby feels abandoned and misses love, security or compassion. In a healthy situation, the following normally occurs:

- The child perceives a deficiency: They need to be held, they need food or want to play.
- The child lets the environment know that they feel this need. They scream or hang on to the skirt of mother.
- A significant person interprets the signal and fulfils the need.

Fortunately, this happens very often, but it is also possible that parents ignore or reject the child's signals. The mother does not offer anything to eat or has no time to play. The child's need is not met. The child's signal then becomes stronger and usually louder. If the caregiver repeatedly ignores or rejects the child's signals, energy is bound up. This happens in different forms:

- The child's perception freezes in the moment of rejection. A part of the child's life energy is bound in an energetic image of the person who does not meet their needs. This image then remains stored in the child's personal space long after the event.
- Energy is not only bound in the perception of the child. The same happens with the reactions to the experienced rejection. Not only physical tension and emotions like sadness, shame and anger are stored in the energy system, but also limiting beliefs and conclusions are created, like "I am not important," "People don't accept my emotions," or "The world is loveless."
- It is also possible that parents are not happy with their response to the needs of the child. The child activates old emotions of guilt, shame or anger in them. They then leave parts of this bound energy as energy structures in the personal space of the child.

The experiences of the child are often so overwhelming that the awareness of their Essence is lost. The striving for the fulfilment of physical, emotional and social needs then comes to the fore.

Fortunately, there are many ways to release bound energy and let it flow again. Later in this book, I will show you how Logosynthesis can help you to do this.

7.

ENERGY BELONGS TO YOU—OR IT DOESN'T

The condition every art requires is,
not so much freedom from restriction,
as freedom from adulteration
and from the intrusion of foreign matter.

– WILLA CATHER

In the Logosynthesis basic model, energy has a second key characteristic:

Energy belongs to you—or it doesn't.

What does this statement mean? We have already seen that all beings, objects and phenomena in this world exist as vibrational patterns or energy fields. You can perceive them in different ways:

- Your eyes and ears perceive frequencies of light and sound.
- With the help of instruments, you can extend the range of your senses, e.g. with binoculars, radar, X-rays, video, or other media.

41

- Your intuition can absorb and assess the energy of people, groups or places.

We do not perceive all these possible structures or fields. That would quickly overwhelm us. We tend to limit our perception to what we need to fulfill our needs and to live a meaningful life.

Structures in space

In Logosynthesis we assume that the three-dimensional space around us is filled with energy structures—like the tables and chairs in your living room. You can sense these structures and patterns just as you perceive a chair or a table with your senses. You can see, hear, feel, smell, or even taste them. In everyday life, such perceptions are regarded as imaginary, as fantasies. In Logosynthesis we assume that they form unique energy fields in their own right.

Thus, all people, objects, words, concepts, phenomena and events in our lives have specific and individual energy fields. With people and objects, this energy field extends around the material form. You can experience this with the exercise on page 57 in chapter 9. This energy field can be made visible with experimental methods.[2]

All these fields affect you. At the beginning of life, the field of your Self is still more or less intact.

---

[2] E.g. URL: https://www.chi.is/systems-mapping-resources/ 21.05.2020

A newborn baby has a strong, unique energy field that is not yet programed with the words, concepts, ideas, rules, codes, norms and behaviors of human life. After entering the world, the free flow of energy from the core of their being is channeled, stored, and frozen in the form of ever new structures. Every child needs all these structures to orient themselves in space and time. The free energy flow of your Self is bound in space and time. In this way, you slowly create a set of structures that can be compared with a personal museum, filled with people, animals, objects, in the form of memories, fantasies, and beliefs.

If your body or your mind is overwhelmed with the flood of events in your immediate environment, then disturbing or limiting structures can arise. In such a case, energy is bound—in an image of the perceived environment and the physical or psychological reactions to the overwhelming event e.g. when a mother or father slaps a child, the following happens in the child's energy system:

- The child splits energy off the flow coming from Essence and creates a frozen representation of the moment of the slap in their personal space. This image contains the frozen perceptions of the parent: the image of a face distorted with rage, the loud tone of their voice and the touch of a strong hand on their cheek.
- The child reacts physically and psychologically to the slap—physically with pain and tension,

emotionally with fear, sadness, confusion, guilt or shame. The mind of the young child forms unconscious beliefs like "There is something wrong with me," "People do not love me," or "In this world, I cannot trust anyone." These reactions are split off from the flow of the child's life energy and stored as independent energy patterns.

– These frozen representations of events are firmly connected to physical, emotional and cognitive reaction patterns. If something like the slap in the face happens later in life, the childhood memory is reactivated along with the emotional reaction to that first slap.

This separation of life energy from its source is called *dissociation*. This process is not limited to the interruption of the flow of one's own energy. Also, the energy of others is involved. We do not only split off our energy into separate parts: We also absorb the energy of others into our system. In the event of the slap this means:

– The behavior—or even the presence—of the child tempts the parent to cross the line: They strike.

– Their energy is frozen in the confrontation with the child. In anger, they split off that life energy from their own flow. As a result, it's frozen in the child's personal space.

From this scene, an energetic representation of the significant person is created in the personal space of the child. This image contains not only the child's energy but also energy from the field of mother or father—external energy.

This way, the initially homogeneous field of the Self becomes fragmented as the child grows up. Sometimes a veritable patchwork quilt is created.

A part of the life energy continues to flow unhindered as the Free Self in contact with Essence—in the service of your mission. A part is transformed by the mind into constructive patterns: We are aware of who we are, who is with us, what we do and how we do it. This is how we slowly gather exhibits for our own personal museums.

Together, these patterns form a map that helps us find our way in the Matrix. This may be a map with empty spaces and wrong paths or an exact, detailed map of the outside world. If your map provides an adequate representation of your current environment, it will help you to fulfill your mission. If it contains outdated or wrong information, it can lead you astray and hinder you in both finding and completing your mission.

The map is not only built from your energy, it also contains the energy of messages from your environment—descriptions, stories, commands, recommendations, permissions, rules and laws. It defines and controls your person within the Matrix: How you should be and could be.

Once you have driven 30 kilometers per hour too fast and have received a hefty fine, you suddenly react very differently to speed signs: The energy of the Matrix enters and occupies a part of your system.

In our work with Logosynthesis we uncover the patterns that are frozen in space and time. Many of these are linked to historical or imaginary stressful events. In the case study in chapter 11, Cleo unconsciously created a threatening image of her boss, Mark, in her personal space. She reacted to this image with fear and concern as if this image were real and he was there.

Logosynthesis can help you improve and redraw your map. Below is a list of the aspects of reality in which energy can be bound. In the fourth part of this book, I will show you how the flow of energy that's bound in these representations can be restored.

Examples of bound energy:

- Memories describe how reality was.
- Fantasies tell you what is going to happen.
- Beliefs contain what reality is.
- Values tell you what is important.
- Wishes describe what you imagine should or must happen.

- Places are stored as representations of a city, a village, a landscape, a time zone, a room.
- A climate is remembered as warm, cold, dry, rainy, windy.
- Symptoms, diseases and states of the physical body occupy your awareness.
- The body is associated with ideas of what it is, was, could or should be.
- Material objects or phenomena can be represented in your personal space.
- Other people and living beings leave their energy in your personal space.
- The Matrix with its socio-energetic fields holds it all: social, economic, organizational, political, cultural, national or continental energy patterns.

Logosynthesis understands dissociated parts and frozen images of the inner and outer realities of human beings as energy structures in three-dimensional space in time. They are not just abstract, cognitive contents of consciousness. These structures are created from the energy of all concerned and can be strengthened, weakened, neutralized or dissolved.

The basic assumptions of Logosynthesis take some getting used to. However, they offer a coherent explanation for all its methods and effects.

8.

WORDS MOVE ENERGY

A song is sleeping in all things
It's dreaming on and on,
and the world will start to sing
once you hit the magic word.

– JOSEPH VON EICHENDORFF

The Power of Words

Energy has two key characteristics in the Logo-synthesis model: It's either frozen or in flow, and it either belongs to you, or it doesn't. The third basic assumption contains the key working principle of Logosynthesis:

Words move energy.

When the world begins to sing, you are in contact with your deepest being, with your Essence. How do you find the magic word in a whole world of words?

The prevailing Western way of thinking regards words as a means of describing the world and putting it into terms—in poetry and prose, technology and science. This is only one aspect though: words have always been more than a tool for naming or understanding reality.

Many spiritual traditions are aware of a mystical connection between words and creation, will and growth. Whoever pronounces the right words causes something specific to happen, an intention. Creation, healing and magic take place through the word. This is how God speaks in the Old Testament (Gen 1:3):

Let there be light.
And there was light.

The Gospel of John in the New Testament begins with:

In the beginning was the Word, and the Word was with God and the Word was God.

Jesus says to the paralyzed man (Mark 2:11):

I tell you, get up, take your mat and go home.

This power of words does not only exist in Christianity. It also exists in other religions. The Quran says in verse (6:73):

When Allah decides something, he just speaks:
Let it be, and it is.

You probably know the spell *Abracadabra*. But did you also know that it is derived from the Aramaic expression *Avrah ka davra* and what it means?

I create by speaking.

Clear words focus the will of the speaker in these examples and thus shape reality. The speaker doesn't need to make great efforts. He says one sentence and it happens. This is not only true for the Creator and His messenger. The formative power of words also has a tradition among people. They pray to connect with a higher being to change their life for the better, they pronounce a blessing or cast a spell on someone, and they curse each other intending to harm. Some people can make warts disappear with one word. A Japanese woman wrote to me that in her culture, every word has its own soul, a Kotodama 言霊.[3] It's easy to imagine something underneath, like Gertrude Stein:

A rose is a rose is a rose.

In the dominant fields of Western culture, the awareness of this formative power of words has been lost. It does not fit into the materialist, deterministic paradigm of science.

---

[3] https://en.wikipedia.org/wiki/Kotodama

Words in Logosynthesis

The real power of Logosynthesis lies in accessing and using the power of words, as we know this from the cultural and religious history of humanity. Once you're willing to accept that the creative power of words exists, you'll become able to use it as an instrument to dissolve frozen energy patterns—to remove blocks and activate dormant resources. To this end, you can say certain sentences that you will get to know in part III of this book. Painful memories fade, fears disappear, and the belief in your own potential returns or become conscious for the first time.

Once you realize how Logosynthesis works and that it works, it will become a key approach in your practice of healing and development for yourself or for others. You reconnect to Essence, you discover your mission in this life, and you remove blocks on your life path. You learn to put the energy of your body, your mind and your Essence into the service of your life's mission. Your Free Self takes on a clear form with a clear intention. You can go through this process partly on your own, but it may be more fruitful to get help from others, especially if you're suffering from loneliness and abandonment in your life: You're not alone. If you are trained as a professional, you can learn to apply Logosynthesis to support your clients with their issues.

How does Logosynthesis work?

On the one hand, Logosynthesis supports people in returning split-off energy to their Free Self. On the other hand, it teaches how to move the energy of accepted values, convictions, emotions and behaviors to where it comes from or where it can no longer do any harm.

For this purpose, you must realize that your emotions, beliefs and thoughts, which you perceive as real, are nothing but thought forms. You create these thought forms from your energy and reactivate them again and again.

The first step to healing is to retrieve your own energy that is bound in a symptom, an emotion or a belief. In a second step, return energy from the outside world that is connected with the disturbing object to its origins. This also happens in a linguistic form. Finally, you retrieve any energy bound in your reactions to the object.

Many counseling and therapy methods originate from biology and psychology. They hardly attribute healing or a manifesting effect to the word itself and use language as an instrument for describing reality and for indirectly influencing the clients' own and foreign worlds—by conditioning, interpretation, trance induction, anchoring or reframing.

In Logosynthesis we have developed our own specific methods and techniques for healing and development through the power of words. With the help of carefully formulated sentences, blocks on your life path are resolved and resources are activated. Distressing thought forms dissolve, and the energy bound up in them becomes fully available. This healing process is very profound: The resolution of long-stored frozen structures allows your Free Self to take the stage and do what needs to be done in the service of your mission.

The Logosynthesis sentences have a tangible effect. After a successful intervention, the atmosphere in the room changes, it becomes quiet in a special way: Traffic noises are muffled, and the tweeting of birds suddenly becomes audible. Diana suffered from a fear of a complex operation. After my Logosynthesis session with her, she wrote me a grateful letter:

> It is now Sunday evening and I haven't had a crying attack or any other kind of emotional collapse since yesterday afternoon. Fantastic! Every now and then I think about the fact that the surgery is imminent—and nothing dramatic happens anymore. I have the impression that the sentences are still floating and spreading in my body, establishing themselves. The process is not yet complete for my perception, but the 'drama' is almost gone—the facts gain the upper hand.

Normally a treated condition does not return in its original form. However, it is quite common for new, deeper aspects of dissociated states to emerge. These are always approached with the same procedure. The process is not always pleasant. There are two reasons for this:

- You suddenly discover that you lack important skills or abilities.

  Eric discovered that he had always stayed out of conflicts or submitted to the wishes of his opponent. When he resolved this pattern, he realized that he missed skills to deal with conflicts. He had to attend a course to learn how to state his opinion in a convincing way.

  Florence didn't believe that she could finish her thesis. She was able to give up this limiting belief, but now she had to learn how to write a coherent text. In the face of a new challenge, old patterns of powerlessness are reactivated. Once these are resolved, it becomes clear that the person must accept the responsibility to learn what's necessary to reach their goals in the present. The resolution usually shows resources in the environment also: Eric could attend a course and Florence could get advice from an experienced friend.

- Resolving a frozen structure allows you to let go of annoying inner dialogues, but it can also lead to an inner silence that can become an oppressive emptiness. In the beginning, the emptiness can seem threatening—until you start to hear the gentle, soft music of your Essence through it. Therefore, dealing with the emptiness can be the reason for a further step in your development. This process can take a while before you learn to recognize your inner voice, your calling, and to be able to implement it in your everyday life.

The life energy of a person can be bound in many different forms and ways. The power of words releases this bound energy and makes it available to your Free Self—in the service of your mission in this life. In the next part of this book, I will describe how to make this possible. In the last part, you will find examples of how to apply Logosynthesis in many different areas.

By now you may be curious how you can learn to use the power of words and to restore the flow of your life energy, but first you'll do an exercise to explore your personal space.

9.

YOUR PERSONAL SPACE—AN EXERCISE

I take the invasion of
my personal space
very seriously.

– KID ROCK

You are energy—Essence manifested as body and mind. Your body is an energy system embedded in a personal space in time. Your space stores many kinds of information, not only about yourself but also about other people, animals and objects. This space is like a museum of all your perceptions, memories, fantasies and beliefs. If energy patterns stored there are in the way of your development, you can neutralize or dissolve them with the help of the Logosynthesis sentences.

Now explore your personal space using the following steps:

– Find a place where you can move freely within a radius of about 5 meters—indoors or outdoors.

- Stand in the middle of this free space and explore the limits of your personal space by answering the following questions:
  - *How big is your personal space?*
  - *Where does it stop? Left, right, up, down, in front of you, behind you?*
  - *Can you recognize the boundaries of your space? How?*
  - *How does this personal space differ from the wider environment?*

Now imagine an important person in the room, e.g. your father, mother, sister or brother.

- *Where do you perceive this person in the room? Left, right, up, down, front, back?*
- *How do you perceive the presence of this person?*
- *Do you see, hear or feel them?*
- *How does your space change when the person is in it?*
- *How do you react to the presence of this person?*
- *Physically? Emotionally?*

Now imagine this person in a different place in the room, in a different direction or at a different distance.

- *How does the quality of your space change when the person is at a different point?*
- *How does your reaction to the person change?*

You can also do the exercise together with a person you trust. It is often interesting to see how different the answers to the individual questions are. Some people experience their personal space as wide, almost without boundaries, while others perceive the border of the space very close to their own body and even feel trapped.

This exercise helps you to expand your awareness of the energy fields of yourself and others. If you do the exercise with others or in a larger group, you can also examine how the fields of different people affect each other. This experience is very useful when you learn to use Logosynthesis.

Part III.

THE LOGOSYNTHESIS BASIC PROCEDURE

**There's no reason
not to follow your heart.**

– STEVE JOBS

Logosynthesis enables you to resolve disturbing energy patterns and to restore the flow of your life energy. This happens in the following steps:

1. You identify blocks in the flow of your life energy in the form of disturbing emotions, physical symptoms, limiting thoughts and resulting behavior patterns.
2. You recognize energy patterns in space that lead to these reactions.
3. You use the power of words to dissolve this disturbing frozen pattern and restore your contact with Essence.

The procedure contains three precisely formulated sentences, each of which has a goal:

1. The person who is bound in the disturbing pattern takes back their energy from the disturbing energy pattern.
2. The person removes energy of other people, animals or objects trapped in the pattern.
3. The person takes back their energy, which is bound in their reactions to this pattern.

After triggering energy patterns or structures have been neutralized, the person's reactions to them also change, and the process moves on to the next phase. If the suffering as a result of a frozen pattern has been sufficiently reduced, a fourth sentence follows. After that, the person can more adequately relate to the situation in the present, and the Basic Procedure of Logosynthesis is complete.

As a rule, energy blocks contain many aspects, both in the frozen perceptions that trigger a person's reactions, as well as in the character of these reactions. When blocks are removed, alternatives show up and possibilities for change arise. If you work with the Logosynthesis model regularly, it deepens your awareness of your Essence, and your life task will start to guide your thoughts and actions in your daily life.

This part of the book offers an introduction to the Basic Procedure, the most important method in the Logosynthesis model. The beginning of this part consists of an exercise and the description of a typical application, using the story of a client: Cleo, as an example. This is followed by an explanation of the individual steps in the Basic Procedure:

- tuning in
- the meta-questions A and B
- the scale for the level of distress
- the sentences with their working pauses
- reassessment and closure.

10.

WHO IS SITTING IN THE CHAIR—AN EXERCISE

**For me, the future is just a
huge bunch of discoveries.**

– AUDREY TAUTOU

This chapter shows how Logosynthesis works with the help of an exercise in two parts. The first one shows the effect of an energetic representation of a person in your space.

Part 1: An encounter with a pleasant person

In the first step of the exercise in chapter 9, you have explored your personal space. Now sit down on a chair in the middle of this space and examine your inner state for a moment:

– *Are you quiet, relaxed, tense, or irritated?*
– *If there is distress in your current situation, how would you rate it on a scale from 0 to 10? 0 means no distress and 10 the highest level possible.*

Now, imagine a person you really like, as if they were present in the space around you. Explore this imaginary presence further:

- *Do you see this person, do you have an image?*
- *Do you hear this person's voice?*
- *Do you feel any physical contact?*
- *Where do you perceive this person in the room? In front of you or behind you? More to the left or right of you? Above or below you? How far away?*

Now put a chair in the place in the room where you perceive this person to be, sit back in your own chair and continue to explore:

- *How do you react to this person? What sensations do you feel in your body? Which emotions do you feel? What are your thoughts about this person?*
- *On the scale 0 to 10 above, how does your experience change when you let their presence take effect?*

If you really like the person and they are close to you, their imagined presence will do you good and reduce your distress level. If distress increases, you can continue the exercise with the representation of this person in part 2. You can also find another person for that part if you prefer.

Part 2: The encounter with an annoying or disturbing person

People are not always pleasant, and you probably have to live with the fact that this is also true for you. Some people you have a hard time with, and you simply cannot get along with them. The second part of this exercise helps you to change or resolve the energy structure of such a person in your personal space. This shift will allow you to react from a more neutral perspective.

For this purpose, imagine a person X, who has recently annoyed or disturbed you, as if they were present in your personal space. Like in part 1, examine this imagery more closely:

– *Do you see this person; do you have an image?*
– *Do you hear this person's voice?*
– *Do you feel any physical contact?*
– *Where do you perceive this person in the room? In front of you or behind you? More to the left or right of you? Above or below you? How far away?*
– *Which part of your perception is most important? The image, the voice or the sensation?*

Now put a chair in the place in the room where you perceive this person to be, sit back in your own chair and continue to explore:

– *How do you react to this person? What sensations do you feel in your body? Which emotions do you feel? What are your thoughts about this person?*
– *How high is the level of distress in your reaction to the imagined presence of X on a scale from 0 to 10?*

Make a note of the level of distress from 0 to 10. You are now focused on this person X and you have examined your perception of this person. You have also explored how you react to this perception and you have assessed the level of distress triggered by this perception. These are the first steps of the Logosynthesis Basic Procedure.

In the next step you neutralize the disturbing image, voice, or sense of X with the help of the first of the three sentences. Therefore, you find a *trigger*, the most significant aspect of the representation you have found in the exploration above. This trigger can be a facial expression, the posture of a person, a voice, another sound, or an unpleasant touch. A trigger is always a perception—something you can see, hear, sense, smell or taste.

You use this most important quality of the perception of X that you identified above, in the sentences 1, 2, and 3 of the Basic Procedure. You say these sentences in a calm voice, without any special emphasis, one at a time and in the right order. After speaking each sentence, you let it sink in until you notice a shift or until a few minutes have passed.

The sentences are:

1. *I retrieve all my energy bound up in this (image, voice, touch, etc.) of X and I take it to the right place in my Self.*

Let this sentence take effect, and observe what happens.

2. *I remove all non-me energy related to this (image, voice, touch, etc.) of X, from all of my cells, all of my body and from all of my personal space and I send it to where it truly belongs.*

Let this sentence take effect, and observe the effect.

3. *I retrieve all my energy bound up in all my reactions to this (image, voice, touch, etc.) of X, and I take it to the right place in my Self.*

Let this sentence work, and observe what happens.

After the third pause you answer the following questions:

– *What has changed in your perception of X: in the image, in the voice?*
– *What has changed in your reactions to the representation of X now? In your body? In your emotions? In your thoughts?*
– *How high is your distress level now on the scale from 0 to 10?*

When we do this exercise in our seminars, participants notice all kinds of changes in their perception of the less than pleasant person X, in their reaction to X, or in the distress triggered by the representation of X in space.

You have now received a first impression of the working method of Logosynthesis. In the following chapter, we describe an example from practice: working with Cleo.

11.

THE CASE OF CLEO

Don't wait for others to light your fire.
You have your own matches.

– ANONYMOUS

Cleo meets the boss

Cleo is a 26-year-old marketing assistant. She has been with the company for two years and loves her job, even though it is a great challenge for her. One morning she receives an e-mail from her boss, Mark. He invites her to an urgent meeting next Friday—without further explanation.

When she reads the message, she starts to worry and becomes restless. In the hours afterwards, she cannot concentrate on her tasks. Scenes appear in her mind in which Mark yells at her or even dismisses her. When she becomes aware of these thought patterns, she sees an opportunity to apply Logosynthesis—which she has recently learned in a workshop. Cleo takes time to focus on the subject, pours herself a glass of water and turns off the phone. Then she examines the details associated with her concerns, and asks herself the following questions:

- *What's happening in my body right now?*
- *What emotions does this trigger in me?*
- *Which thoughts keep popping up?*
- *On a scale from 0 to 10, how distressing is this experience?*

Cleo notices that she feels a tightness in her throat and stomach. She is anxious and keeps imagining that her boss will fire her. When she thinks of next Friday, the stress level is 8 on the scale from 0 to 10.

Then Cleo examines what it is that triggers this stress. She explores her fantasies about the coming meeting and concentrates on the worst she can imagine: The boss yells at her and tells her the company doesn't need her anymore and that she has to leave immediately. Again, she asks herself questions:

- *Who or what is the most important thing in this scene?*
  The image of her angry, yelling boss.
- *Where in the space around me do I perceive him to be?*
  The boss is standing right in front of Cleo.
- *Do I see it, hear it or sense it?*
  Cleo sees the reddened face of her boss, she hears his loud voice and she senses his strong energy.

Now Cleo designs sentence 1 of the Logosynthesis Basic Procedure and says it aloud. This sentence helps her to take back her energy which is bound up in the image, sound and sensation of the fantasy that her boss is firing her.

1. *I retrieve all my energy, bound up in this image of my boss firing me, and I take it to the right place in my Self.*

After she has said the sentence in a normal voice and without special emphasis, Cleo lets the words sink in. In this pause, she only observes what happens inside her. After 30-40 seconds she notices that she relaxes a bit. She continues with sentence 2:

2. *I remove all non-me energy, related to this image of my boss firing me, from all of my cells, from all of my body and from all of my personal space, and I send it to where it truly belongs.*

Again, Cleo lets the sentence take effect and observes what happens during the pause. A minute passes, she breathes deeply and notices that her shoulders are more relaxed. Her neck feels good and she slowly calms down. Now she formulates sentence 3, which retrieves her energy that is bound in her reactions to the imagined scene:

3. *I retrieve all my energy, bound up in all my reactions to this image of my boss firing me, and I take it to the right place in my Self.*

Again, she pauses and observes. She feels relaxed, her stomach is free, and she feels her life energy starting to flow. Something interesting has happened: Instead of being afraid of the angry boss in her fantasy and trying to avoid him, Cleo realizes that Mark, her manager, is himself stressed out and overwhelmed by his responsibility. He needs her support to be able to carry his workload.

With this insight, she drinks a glass of water and goes back to work, relaxed. The meeting next Friday will be a perfect opportunity to take responsibility and show Mark her commitment.

What happened here?

Logosynthesis helped Cleo to let go of inappropriate reaction patterns and to find her way back to her competence. After being anxious, tense and confused at first, she became able to understand Mark's point of view and to reconcile it with her own.

This case is typical when Logosynthesis is applied directly to events on the surface of our consciousness. Cleo encounters an everyday challenge when preparing for the meeting with Mark. She does not feel able to deal with this situation. Her reaction pattern contains the following steps:

- *She creates a fantasy movie of her meeting with Mark.*
- *She reacts to this fantasy with destructive thoughts, strong emotions and physical tension.*

Using self-coaching, Cleo is able to explore this imaginary movie as well as her reactions to it. She says three sentences, each followed by a pause. During this pause, she observes what is going on inside her. This procedure immediately changes her thoughts, emotions and physical sensations: The new imagery of the meeting and the associated reactions are neutral, and she is able to think, feel and act adequately.

This is a common result of applying Logosynthesis to a distressing fantasy. Does this make you curious?

The role of images

The application of the Logosynthesis Basic Procedure results in a change in the fantasy movie of Cleo's boss and her reactions to it. This change enables an appropriate response to the current challenge. Cleo's fantasy about how Mark will behave is an example of how we create images of the world around us every day—in terms of past, present and future. It is a strategy that enables us to understand and predict events in the Matrix. We compare our present environment with our memories and create images of the future. In this way, we learn from experience and anticipate problems to be solved.

However, conclusions can also be disturbing when we encounter new challenges. Cleo's frame of reference activates a threatening fantasy. The Logosynthesis Basic Procedure helps her to rethink perceptions, emotions and fantasies in a way that supports her mission. Her thinking becomes creative; her emotions change from fear and anxiety to a calm self-confidence. The power of words activates the energy of her Free Self.

Words work wonders

By examining her situation, constructing three sentences, speaking them, and letting them take effect, Cleo is able to change her attitude towards Mark and the upcoming meeting. Her emotional and physical reactions also change abruptly. This paves the way for a different behavior: If Cleo can perceive her boss as a stressed manager, she can meet him calmly and even support him.

In the next chapters, we will examine each step Cleo has taken in this example.

12.

TUNING IN

I'm not lost, for I know where I am.
But, however, where I am may be lost.

– WINNIE THE POOH

Preparation
With some experience, you can apply the Logo-synthesis Basic Procedure in almost any situation. The best way, however, is to find a quiet place, switch off your phone and have a bottle of water ready. If you work professionally with clients, as a coach, counselor or a psychotherapist, you can easily integrate the Basic Procedure into the flow of a session. My Logosynthesis Handbook for the Helping Professions gives detailed information about this.[4]

Getting in the mood for an issue
Life in the present is often interrupted, hindered or blocked by a myriad of energy patterns and our reactions to them. Like in a personal museum, we collect frozen memories, fantasies and beliefs that change our perception of reality like a scratched lens

---

[4]   The books are listed in the appendix.

might. Sometimes, people have so many statues in their virtual museum that they are constantly caught up in memories from the past or in fantasies about the future. They are not able to assess what's really going on in everyday reality.

The best way to explore these frozen worlds is to observe your thoughts, emotions, memories and fantasies. Each day offers opportunities to recognize and dissolve disturbing patterns. You can apply the Logosynthesis Basic Procedure at any time and for any form of disturbance or suffering.

Sometimes, as in the case of Cleo, you concentrate on a certain scene, person or object and neutralize it. On other occasions, you find only the tip of the iceberg and the problem turns out to imply many more aspects. In such a situation, you proceed step by step, like Thomas in chapter 16. It's like eating artichokes: layer by layer until you get to the heart.

I recommend working in small steps and not trying to solve everything at once. After each step, your body and your mind need time to adjust to the more intensive flow of energy: The gradual reorganization of your energy system is just as important as the release of any blocks that you may have.

Assessment of distress

When you have identified an issue, you start the Basic Procedure by examining the triggers and reactions connected to the issue. We use a SUD scale

(*Subjective Units of Distress*) to assess a level between 0 and 10. At a zero, the issue is completely neutral, and you feel no distress at all. At 10, the distress level is extremely high. There is no such thing as 11!

The SUD scale helps you to recognize differences before and after saying the sentences. This is useful because the state after the sentences sometimes feels so natural that the degree of change is not noticed at all. Even if the first three sentences do not completely resolve the issue, this is helpful: You can then notice the differences before and after a cycle of sentences and adjust the content of the sentences accordingly.

The SUDs do not have to be reduced to zero. Even a reduction from 9 to 6 can help you to see the issue differently and to find the courage to take another step.

There are two sets of important questions that help to create the content of the sentences accurately and precisely. The worksheet in the appendix on page 179 will help you to clarify them.

A recommendation

Many people have experienced very painful life events and have had to deal with it without any help from others. If you are suffering from a problem that has existed for a long time, do find a psychotherapist or a counselor. These professionals are trained to offer a safe environment and to support you in overcoming blocks on the path to new meaning in your life. You don't need to resolve everything on your own now, even though that's been your experience in the past.

13.

THE META-QUESTIONS

The truth is in the details.

– STEPHEN KING

When an issue holds you captive, you can't think clearly. You are overwhelmed by painful emotions or symptoms—you suffer. All kinds of things are going through your mind and you don't know how to escape from it. Such a stressful condition is often the starting point for working with the Logosynthesis Basic Procedure.

Suffering binds energy. Under stress, your brain only knows fight, flight, freeze, fawn, and faint. To find effective sentences and to reduce stress, you need a certain distance from the issues involved. To create this distance, I have developed the meta-questions. These are key questions that enable the transition from the experience of distress to the state necessary to create and speak the sentences of Logosynthesis.

There are two sets of meta-questions. They help you to clarify the issue and find keywords for the

Logosynthesis sentences. The work with the meta-questions is done in two steps:

1. The first step, meta-question A: *How do you suffer?* helps you to explore your current state. You are sad, anxious, confused, annoyed or angry, ashamed or feel guilty. Meta-question A helps you to investigate this suffering in detail. This also helps you to see a difference after applying the sentences. It is not necessary to stay in this state: As soon as you have found words for the symptoms and suffering, you move on to meta-question B. You only return to the experience to check how the sentences have worked. This is different from many other methods which keep the experience of suffering in the foreground for a longer time.

2. The second step, meta-question B, demands a certain distance: *What makes you suffer?* What makes you anxious, sad or angry? Is it a memory, a specific event, or a belief? The answer to meta-question B opens a new perspective on the issue. It detaches you from the emotions and symptoms and allows you to reflect on their origin. The answer to meta-question B is the key for the content of the sentences.

In the transition from meta-question A to meta-question B, you need to change your perspective. You move away from the emotions, sensations, and symptoms and find out what leads to the suffering. Because suffering and its triggers are often closely linked, this change is a challenge, especially in the beginning. As a rule, the answers to meta-question A tend to be more emotional and the answers to meta-question B more factual.

Meta-question A: the symptom and the suffering

Meta-question A examines the complaints, difficulties and symptoms you suffer from. You ask a series of questions. Meta question A in short form is:

HOW DO YOU SUFFER?

The underlying group of questions explores the nature of suffering in your body and mind. Examples are:

- *What happens in my body when I concentrate on the problem? Do I feel pain, tension, heat, cold or a tremor? Where in my body do I feel this?*
- *What emotions do I feel?*
- *What thoughts keep running through my head?*
- *How high is my distress level on a scale from 0 to 10?*

After answering meta-question A, you reassess the level of distress you are currently experiencing on a scale from 0 to 10. In most cases, this second assessment is more precise than the tuning in described in chapter 12.

Meta-question B: the trigger

The answer to meta-question A described the way in which you are suffering. As you will discover when you continue learning Logosynthesis, experiences of suffering are very often reactions to *triggers*: memories, fantasies, or beliefs that are stored as frozen energy patterns.

Many approaches for personal change and development try to resolve reactions; they do not address the triggers of the disturbing state. Logosynthesis focuses on the latter—it examines and neutralizes the triggers, and that means that the reactions in the form of distress also disappear. These triggers can have a long history, as with Thomas in chapter 16. Meta-question B is designed to identify the triggers you can use as keywords in the sentences of the Logosynthesis Basic Procedure. The short form of meta-question B is:

WHAT MAKES YOU SUFFER?

In meta-question B you concentrate on representations of people and things in your personal space. It includes questions such as:

– *If someone or something were to cause or trigger these reactions, who or what would it be?*
– *Where in the room is this person or thing? On the left? On the right? In front of or behind you? Above or below you? How far away?*

How do you know that you perceive that person or thing there? Do you see, hear, feel, smell or taste them?

The answer to meta-question B contains a concrete perception or representation: You see a person, you hear a voice, you feel or touch, you smell a scent, or you taste something. It is exactly this representation that triggers the emotions and body reactions that you suffer from. It's important to find a clear description of the trigger to use in your Logosynthesis sentences.

Examples of triggers are the picture of Cleo's boss in chapter 11 or Thomas' teacher in chapter 16.

When you have found the trigger, give it a name such as "Mark's Face," "Mr. Jones' voice," or "the laughter of the classmates." Make sure that the name you find for the trigger is based on perception: You must be able to see, hear, feel, smell or taste it. Now you can apply the sentences of Logosynthesis and experience the power of words.

When you are trapped in suffering, you often cannot see the bigger picture. This usually only becomes clear through your answers to meta-question B.

14.

SENTENCES AND
WORKING PAUSES

> He was always in a hurry
> to get where he was not.
>
> – LEO TOLSTOY

Now you have collected enough material to apply your first sequence of the sentences of the Logosynthesis Basic Procedure. One sequence contains three standard sentences. Sometimes you will use a fourth sentence at the end of the procedure (see page 94). The sentences are:

1. *I retrieve all my energy bound up in X* (memory, fantasy, belief or aspect of this), and I take it to the right place in myself.
2. *I remove all non-me energy related to X* (memory, fantasy, belief or aspect of this), *from all of my cells, all of my body and all of my personal space and I send it to where it truly belongs.*

3. *I retrieve all my energy bound up in all my reactions to X*
   (perception, fantasy, belief or aspect of this),
   and I take it to the right place in my Self.

X is a concrete perception, a representation of the reality you experience with any of your five senses, as described in chapter 13. X may be:

- *visual*: a face, a teacup, or a landscape.
- *auditory*: a voice, music, or an explosion.
- *kinesthetic/tactile*: a physical sensation such as the wind, the cold on your skin or a slap.
- *olfactory*: the smell of perfume or a fire burning.
- *gustatory*: the taste of pepper or pizza.

Even though there are other ways to formulate the content of the sentences, I recommend formulating X as a concrete perception only, especially at the beginning of your Logosynthesis experience.

Before you start a sequence, check again that what you are going to say meets the criteria for a well-formed sentence:

- The sentence contains a clear and succinct description of a situation that is real or imagined.
- The sentence ideally contains only one concrete perception: an image, a smell, a sound/voice, a touch, a taste, or a smell.
- The perception either refers to a past situation or contains a fantasy that causes future distress, or it

relates to something that could or should have happened.

- Emotions like fear, anger, grief, guilt, and shame never appear in the sentences. They are reactions to the trigger; they are not the trigger. In the sentences, we address the frozen perceptions of only the trigger. Distress in its different forms is automatically neutralized in the third sentence. There is no need to mention emotional states directly.
- If you are dealing with a belief, address it as words you read on a page or as a voice you hear saying the words of that belief.

Say the sentences

In the beginning, when you learn the Logosynthesis Basic Procedure, you pronounce each sentence calmly, at normal volume and without any intonation. This helps you focus on the process: If you say the sentences out loud, you won't be thinking of something else at the same time. If the sentences gradually become more familiar, you can whisper them or even just think them.

Sentence 1

Sentence 1 helps you to retrieve your life energy that is blocked in frozen perceptions, ideas or beliefs and that is leading to the disturbing reactions you want to address. The X in the sentence is the trigger you found in meta-question B. This is summarized in a keyword or a short sentence:

1. *I retrieve all my energy bound up in X*
    (perception, fantasy, belief, or an aspect of this),
    and I take it to the right place in my Self.

Now you pause, relax and let the sentence take effect. You can close your eyes while doing this. Wait until a few minutes have passed, until you feel a shift: Your eyes open spontaneously, or you notice a change in your body or your emotions. Take your time.

Sentence 2

Images of fantasies and memories contain not only your own energy, but also energy of other people and things. By simply saying sentence 2, you remove this energy from your field through the power of words. Again, the keyword X in the sentence is the trigger from meta-question B:

2. *I remove all non-me energy related to X*
    (perception, fantasy, belief, or aspect of this),
    from all of my cells, from all of my body and from all of my personal space
    and I send it to where it truly belongs.

Pause again, relax and observe. Take your time to let the words sink in. Wait until a few minutes have passed or until you notice a shift in your body or your emotions. If you become distracted or your mind wanders, just return to the issue you are working with.

Sentence 3

In meta-question A, you focused on suffering, and you recognized your reactions to representations that trigger you. In the third sentence, the energy that is bound in these reaction patterns is returned to your Self.

3. *I retrieve all my energy bound up in all my reactions to X*
   (perception, fantasy, belief, or aspect of this),
   and I take it to the right place in my Self.

Pause again, relax and watch what happens. Wait patiently until a few minutes have passed or until you feel a shift in your body or emotions. Don't rush the process.

The working pause

After each sentence, you take some time to let it sink in and be processed. This working pause can take from 30 seconds to 10 minutes; sometimes even longer. Usually the material is processed more deeply when you allow more time for the process after saying a sentence. In my work with clients, I have also experienced even longer working pauses. In the beginning though, they tend to be shorter.

During the pause and while you are processing, you can close your eyes to avoid external influences and disturbances. During this pause, the best thing you can do is just observe. Active reflection or an inner dialogue will slow down the process. If you feel tired, dizzy, or nauseous, drink a glass of water. When your eyes open or the processing feels finished, you continue with the next sentence.

15.

REASSESSMENT
AND CONCLUSION

**We have somehow conned ourselves into
the notion that this moment is ordinary.**

– ALAN WATTS

In this step, you compare your state of mind with
your answers to the meta-questions A and B on your
worksheet. Then you reassess your experienced level
of distress on the scale from 0 to 10.

After this, the next step is to look into the
future—we call this *future pacing*. Neutralizing a
painful memory, a disturbing fantasy, or a limiting
belief, has an immediate effect on how you will think
and feel about your future. Say the sentences and let
them work. Then imagine a similar situation in the
future. If you stay relaxed with this new fantasy, you
will be able to notice and compare your thoughts
and emotions to how they were before you said the
sentences. Pay attention to your body, your thoughts
and the strength of your reactions: What has
changed? What is different now? How is it different?

If blocks or disturbances still occur, you can process them in another sequence of the Logosynthesis Basic Procedure. Answer the meta-questions again, formulate new sentences, say them and let them take effect. Each sequence can be followed by another one if needed. I recommend a maximum time limit of 40 minutes per session. It is important to allow your energy system to adjust and find a new balance.

Sentence 4

The fourth sentence is the icing on the cake of Logosynthesis. You pronounce it after the issue you have worked on feels resolved, and you have reached a new level of awareness and relaxation in your life. You can see life problems as challenges instead of being overwhelmed by them. In this case, you'll probably rate the distress caused by the issue as 0 to 3 on the SUD scale. This is the moment to say sentence 4:

4. *I attune all my systems to this new awareness.*

Again, pause, relax and observe. Wait patiently until a few minutes have passed or you notice a change. This sentence concludes the Logosynthesis process for the moment.

The layers of the onion

Our experience shows that behind every aspect that you work on, there are new and deeper issues underneath. That is part of life, and you can process them all with the sentences, on your own or with the help of a professional. For many people, Logosynthesis becomes a daily practice, like meditation, fitness or yoga. It supports your personal and spiritual development. The effect and new freedom that you will experience is quickly noticeable, and the newly flowing energy is available for you to use—making processing more difficult issues that much easier.

In applying Logosynthesis, sometimes hidden, frozen worlds are activated. This process can lead to intense emotions and physical symptoms. Not everyone can perceive these frozen worlds for what they are: blocked energy. If this happens to you, please seek help. The website of the Logosynthesis International Association (LIA), offers a list of trained and certified professionals, many of whom also offer their services online.[5]

---

[5]   http://www.logosynthesis.international/professionals/

Part IV.

APPLYING LOGOSYNTHESIS

**Now I know refuge never grows
from a chin in a hand in a thoughtful pose.
Gotta tend the earth if you want a rose.**

– INDIGO GIRLS

In the first and second parts of this book, I have presented the framework and the energy concept of Logosynthesis. In the third part, you have learned to apply the Logosynthesis Basic Procedure. Part IV offers a series of approaches to working with a variety of issues.

Symptoms, diagnosis and treatment

In traditional science, the diagnosis of a disorder concentrates on symptoms or groups of symptoms that lead to suffering. Symptoms can be biological and related to organs or functions. They can be psychological, focusing on mental and emotional states or describing a behavior. Usually, a condition is identified by interviewing the client. Also, objective measurements such as temperature, blood pressure, the blood level of certain substances, EEG or ECG are taken. Diagnostic questionnaires are another form of assessment.

A doctor may diagnose asthma, coronary disease, allergy, hereditary disease or a certain type of cancer. A psychologist or psychotherapist can diagnose a client as bipolar, borderline or depressed. They may suffer from a phobia, an addiction, a generalized anxiety disorder or post-traumatic stress disorder (PTSD).

Based on this diagnosis, a treatment starts, which ranges from medication, surgery, radiation or exercise to talking therapy and cognitive behavioral therapy. The treatment is aimed at alleviating or resolving the symptoms. This treatment varies with the professional discipline of the healer. A surgeon will know how to make the right incision, a psychiatrist is more likely to prescribe medication and a psychotherapist will talk with you.

Often clients come to counseling or psychotherapy with a classical diagnosis. Members of our internet forums often ask questions like: "Can Logosynthesis be used to treat X?" X can mean anything from allergies to tinnitus to psychosis to multiple sclerosis.

The answer will never be clear. It always is: "I don't know" or "Yes, but..." The reason for these vague answers is that in the application of

Logosynthesis we rarely work directly from a biological or psychological diagnosis.

In Logosynthesis work, a diagnosis is the starting point to examine the person as a complex energy system. The key questions to identify blocks in the flow of energy are:

1. Where is energy bound?
2. Does this energy belong to the person's system?

An example: An allergy represents a specific reaction of your organism to an external stimulus. It perceives this stimulus and interprets that it is dangerous—falsely. One could say that your system has a belief that activates your immune system to cause sneezing and watery eye reactions.

The usual medical treatment of an allergy inhibits the unpleasant reaction to the pollen (stimulus) by treating it with antihistamines or even steroids. These medications interrupt the irritant—organism reaction sequence. However, the original misinformation (that pollen is dangerous) remains in your system. If you stop taking the antihistamines, you'll start sneezing again.

Diagnosis and treatment in Logosynthesis

With the help of the Logosynthesis sentences, you can retrieve your energy from the incorrectly programmed information. The relevant program line in your system is deleted and the symptoms disappear: Pollen is no longer perceived as dangerous. Therefore, no defense mechanism is activated, and your mucous membranes will not be irritated anymore. Many people experience an enormous relief of allergic or asthmatic symptoms by retrieving their energy from the flawed programming of their organism, which perceives pollen as dangerous. Today I can walk across a flowering mountain meadow in May, without a trace of the symptoms I used to suffer from for more than half of my life.

This is only the surface of the issue though. The above Logosynthesis approach may be too simplistic. It does not deal with the question of when, how and why the erroneous pattern was programmed into the organism. You may need to examine a deeper layer of the onion and find out if the first symptoms appeared after an accident, the divorce of your parents, the birth of a new sibling, or after another painful experience.

It is therefore not easy to answer the question of whether Logosynthesis works for a specific allergy. It also requires a thorough examination of the energy patterns associated with the symptoms or diagnosis. You need to find out where the frozen energy is bound. Is it in the body, in the mind, in other people, or in the fields of the Matrix?

Application in guided change and self-coaching

At the level of the mind, life in the present is influenced by the repeated mental and emotional patterns that determine how a person deals with their past and their anticipated future. The most important fields of application for Logosynthesis are therefore:

1. Trauma: An injury in the past leads the person to expect similar injuries in the present, and to perceive people and circumstances accordingly.
2. Grief and nostalgia: Good experiences with people or circumstances are not remembered and the present is seen as less valuable than the past.
3. Fear: The future is perceived as uncertain and the person expects pain and injury or loss. Their own abilities to deal with future trouble are judged as insufficient to avert the threatening situation.
4. Hope: The person expects that people and circumstances in the future will be more friendly than today. They may underestimate the importance of their own actions in creating the future changes they want to happen.
5. Disturbing and limiting beliefs: These may also be taken in from the Matrix. If your mother has a fear of mice, you may copy this pattern from her without ever checking if mice are really dangerous.

A wide range of options

The scope of Logosynthesis goes beyond the classical applications of coaching, psychological counseling and psychotherapy. In this part of the book we deal with the following fields of application—without claiming to be complete:

- positive and negative memories
- positive and negative fantasies
- relationships with people and animals
- limiting beliefs and value systems
- addictions and compulsions
- the environment
- the body
- the fields of matter
- the Matrix: society, culture and religion

In this part of the book I will discuss some of these applications in more detail so that you get an idea how to use Logosynthesis for your own issues in everyday life.

My books *Self-Coaching with Logosynthesis* and *Logosynthesis. A Handbook for the Healing Professions*, offer many concrete case examples.

16.

MEMORIES DISTURB THE PRESENT

The past beats inside me
like a second heart.

– JOHN BANVILLE

Thomas presents to the management team

Thomas is a 30-year-old manager in a mechanical engineering company. He is competent, appreciated by his colleagues and his boss. He has worked in the company for seven years and participated in many projects.

Thomas has a problem. Next Monday he will have to present his own project to the management team for the first time. He has worked on it for many months. He is convinced that it is great and that it will bring the company many orders. As the day of the presentation approaches, he gets nervous. He sleeps badly and dreams of the board members throwing eggs and tomatoes at him. Strangely, some of the attackers in the dream are former schoolmates.

He wakes up sweating, with a racing heart. This nightmare comes back twice in one week. In the office, he continues to struggle with the presentation. On Friday evening he even thinks about giving up. His colleagues look at him and wonder what is going on. They do not recognize his plight. After work, Thomas continues to imagine scenarios that match his nightmares. The self-confident Thomas seems to be nothing more than a pale memory.

The next day he takes part in an introductory course in self-coaching with Logosynthesis. As he is under a lot of pressure, Thomas volunteers for a demonstration and asks for support for his upcoming presentation.

I ask him to imagine the scene of the presentation and ask him some questions:

- *What happens in your body?*
- *What emotions does that evoke in you?*
- *What thoughts are you observing?*
- *What's the worst that could happen?*
- *On a scale from 0 to 10, how much does that distress you?*

Thomas reports sweating, heart palpitations, and a knot in his stomach. He is scared and thinks he is a loser. Then the fantasy appears that his boss makes fun of him, that all his colleagues laugh at him and that they call him a loser. His level of distress on the scale from 0 to 10 is a 9: the pressure is really high.

I ask Thomas to explore what he perceives in the space around him. What triggers this intense reaction? In response to my question, Thomas perceives his boss on the right side and his colleagues in a semicircle behind him. As he lets the images emerge, he notices that the knot in his stomach hurts even more.

I formulate the first sentence and ask Thomas to repeat it:

1. *I retrieve all my energy,*
    bound up in this image of the management team
    and the presentation,
    and I take it to the right place in my Self.

Thomas repeats the sentence. He pauses and observes what happens. The knot in his stomach shrinks, and he starts to yawn. We often see this when processing disturbing patterns. Then I give him the second sentence:

2. *I remove all non-me energy,*
    related to this image of the management team and
    the presentation,
    from all of my cells, from all of my body
    and from all of my personal space,
    and I send it to where it truly belongs.

Thomas also repeats this sentence. Again, he takes a deep breath and observes what happens. The knot is still there, but he feels less fear. Then he receives the third sentence:

3. *I retrieve all my energy,*
   bound up in all my reactions
   to this image of the management team and the
   presentation,
   and I take it to the right place in my Self.

Now, something strange happens. Thomas no longer sees his boss and the team. Suddenly there is a picture of a former teacher, Mr. Jones, whom he remembers as a tyrant. He tells me this, and I help him to clarify the picture:

– *How do you know Mr. Jones is there?*
– *Do you see him? Can you hear him? Feel him?*
– *How far away is he?*

Thomas' answers come quickly:

> *Mr. Jones is on my right, about three meters away. He is much taller than me and exposes me in front of the whole class. He is mean, and all the kids make fun of me, and he allows it!*

The first sequence of Logosynthesis sentences has reactivated an old memory. This has been stored in Thomas' system for many years, without ever being processed. Thomas receives sentence 1 for the picture from the past:

1. *I retrieve all my energy,*
    bound up in this picture of Mr. Jones and the
    teasing children,
    and I take it to the right place in my Self.

After saying the sentence, Thomas closes his eyes for a long two minutes. His eyes move quickly behind his closed lids. After a while, he starts to yawn again and breathe deeply. He gets sentence 2:

2. *I remove all non-me energy related*
    to this picture of Mr. Jones and the teasing
    children, from all of my cells, all of my body and
    from all of my personal space,
    and I send it to where it truly belongs.

He pauses and lets the sentence take effect. His face and shoulders relax. When he opens his eyes, he looks peaceful and liberated. The knot in his stomach is gone. His heart feels good, but he still thinks he is a loser, even if with less intensity. He gets sentence 3:

3. *I retrieve all my energy, bound in all my*
    reactions to this picture of Mr. Jones and the
    teasing children, and I take it to the right place
    in my Self.

This time, the processing pause is shorter. After 20 seconds Thomas opens his eyes. He feels calm and confident. Now I change from the past to the future: I ask him to imagine the scene of the presentation next Monday again. Lo and behold, there is no trace of fear or tension. Thomas is calm and confident. As he drinks a large glass of water, he says: *"I'm not afraid anymore. I am even looking forward to the presentation. I have something important to say!"*

Because the presented problem seems to have been resolved, he now receives the fourth sentence:

4. *I attune all my systems to this new awareness.*

Thomas pronounces the sentence and lets it work. He thanks me and goes back to his place in the audience with a big smile on his face.

A few days later he tells me in an e-mail that the presentation has been a huge success. The boss even invited him to lunch.

What happened here?

This case is a typical example of what happens when Logosynthesis is applied at a deeper level than in Cleo's situation. While working with Thomas' dark visions of the future, a painful memory from the classroom emerges. Thomas experiences the same emotions, thoughts and physical reactions in both situations. In the humiliating situation of the past, he was overwhelmed, and nobody had supported him.

The carefully chosen sentences of Logosynthesis eliminate the connection between the present and the disturbing memory of the past. As a result,

Thomas was able to recognize the reality of his present situation. He was able to fully use his adult skills and abilities and thus realize his potential. He's an adult, he's not sitting in the classroom anymore.

17.

FANTASIES BIND ENERGY

Predictions are difficult, especially when they concern the future.

– MARK TWAIN

Imagine a tropical beach, with palm trees swaying, the sound of the waves, a light breeze over your skin and the smell of the sea air. Does this fantasy lead to a pleasant, deep relaxation, or do you immediately think of jam-packed airports, overcrowded beaches and jellyfish in the water?

The world is full of imaginations, wishes, fantasies, expectations, prophecies and dreams. That's a good thing. When you read the menu in a restaurant, when you book a trip or apply for a job: you always create a fantasy of what's coming to you. Imagination is at the base of every decision. This is not only the case when you're planning a holiday, but also when finding a new apartment, a job or a partner.

Without fantasies, you will not make ends meet in this society. You need fantasies to shape your life, to weigh up alternatives and to make a decision. However, scenarios, expectations and fantasies can also restrict you, bind your energy, and cause distress.

Each scenario is connected with an individual reaction. A fantasy in itself says nothing about your reaction. It's just an energy pattern, but it's often automatically linked to a frozen reaction. For some, the idea of a 40-day quarantine is a catastrophe. Others see it as an opportunity to be productive. Before quarantine, it's just a fantasy, and the reaction to this fantasy varies with patterns in your energy system—if your energy is bound or in flow.

Fantasies can refer to the future, to the present and even to the past. They can open up or close off options, depress or motivate, and bind or release energy. You can use Logosynthesis to free energy that is bound in fantasies, scenarios, wishes, hopes and expectations. This clears your mind and allows you to be present and to think realistically.

Fantasies about the future

In chapter 11 Cleo has a fantasy. She creates an energy pattern, an imaginary video of her boss firing her. This pattern leads to anxiety. The application of the Logosynthesis sentences neutralizes the patterns and the stress reaction dissolves. Afterwards, Cleo can perceive Mark in the context of his own challenges. In the case of Cleo, her limiting fantasy leads to distress.

There are also fantasies in which you imagine a future that is rosier than the one that reality will offer you. This is often the case in romantic relationships. You're floating on cloud nine for a while, until the reality of the Matrix overtakes: The dishes must be done, and the garbage taken out. Romantic love has blinded you to the everyday obligations of life as a couple. In chapter 19, we'll look at other ideals that we may create.

Fantasies about the future can also have a constructive component. If you encounter an unsatisfactory situation, you can design a solution and implement it. It can be the redesign of your garden, moving to a new house, or discovering your mission for your life. Logosynthesis can help you to identify and dissolve blocks in your expectations and fantasies.

A little exercise

Think of a situation that follows a pattern that's been annoying you for a long time. Such patterns usually contain two parts: There is something you want to achieve, and something is stopping you from taking the next step: Yes, but… You have a fantasy that it will become worse, if you change something. This "but" is the key to your application of Logosynthesis. Imagine your worst-case scenario, then say the sentences for this fantasy. The fantasy is the X in the sentences. Afterwards, it will be easier to make a decision to make a change. The "but" will no longer be a problem.

Fantasies about the present

Our society invites us to compare. There is your reality and that of your neighbors, friends, and the rich and beautiful. Others have or are something you would like to have or be—or not. A comparison can make you happy or sad. If it depresses you, look for the disturbing images or statements and neutralize them with the Logosynthesis sentences.

Reality can thwart your ideas. When the first lockdown was declared because of COVID-19, I had planned to offer seminars on the Canary Islands, in Baltimore, Maryland, at home and in Berlin. People had registered, hotels were booked, and flights were paid for. Everything looked as if it was really going to happen. However, reality did not match the expectations, and it took me quite a few sequences of the Logosynthesis sentences to come to terms with the unexpected situation. Then, instead of giving seminars, I wrote the books I had wanted to write for years.

Ideas about the present do not only exist in times of a pandemic. Your boss, the city council or the government of your country makes decisions that affect you: simply because you work in the company, live in the city or own the passport of the country. Your ability to influence these decisions is limited. If you don't want to get into politics, you can only write letters to the editor or support a lobby. You are affected but have no influence. You can use Logosynthesis to help you deal with unmet expectations about the influence of people and authorities. If a new law comes into effect, you'll have to follow it, if you like it or not.

Ideas about the past

The past is the past. So, let's forget about it. If it were only that simple! In the chapter on memories, you read that human life energy can be bound up in the past. A frozen perception of past events can lead to stressful reactions in the present. With Logosynthesis you can neutralize these memories. After that, the past is no different, it just will not affect you anymore. There is another way in which the past can lead to problems: by fantasizing about how it could or should have been. Here is the case of Myra:

Myra was involved in a car accident on a large city square. She had been trapped in the car and had experienced terrible pain. She worked through this traumatic experience with me, but the distress level remained high. As I continued to explore the scene with her, a new image appeared. From her unfortunate position in the car wreck, she saw a police patrol just 50 meters away. The police were talking in a relaxed manner, and they didn't take any initiative to help her. She almost choked in indignation because she had received no help in her pain. I gave her the following sentences for the fantasy that the policemen would free her. Pay attention to the special third sentence:

1. *I retrieve all my energy, bound up in the fantasy that the police officers should have freed me, and I take it to the right place in my Self.*
2. *I remove all non-me energy, related to the idea that the policemen should have freed me, from all of my cells, all of my body and from all of my personal space, and I send it to where it truly belongs.*
3. *I retrieve all my energy bound up in all of my reactions to the fact that the policemen did not free me, and I take it to the right place in my Self.*

Myra spoke the sentences and let them work. Then she said, without even a hint of outrage: *"It's true. They should have helped me, but they didn't. Well, I survived."*

18.

BELIEFS BLOCK YOUR THINKING

Whether you believe you can do a thing or not, you are right.

– HENRY FORD

The world around us is incredibly complex. I assume that human intelligence is not enough to understand it in its entirety. Therefore, we have to reduce complexity to find our way, to make decisions and to survive. In the course of our history, we invent, develop, or adopt beliefs. They enable us to understand how the world works and to find our way in it.

Your convictions and beliefs must be meaningful—literally. A meaningful belief keeps you in touch with Essence and helps you to find your way in the Matrix. Meaningful beliefs guide your thinking, your emotions and your behavior. They support you in developing, planning and in carrying out what is important for your life mission.

Meaningful beliefs cover your life as a whole. They relate to you, to your relationship with others, and to life itself. They enable you to assess what is achievable, to reconcile your life with the unattainable. They help to overcome the limitations and the injuries of the past and don't try to rewrite history. They are coherent and appropriate, realistic and they feel good in your body.

That sounds simple—but it is not. Some beliefs support healing and development while others make life more complicated and don't reduce complexity at all! Beliefs bring you closer to your Essence or they alienate you from it. Sometimes there are, as Goethe's Dr. Faustus said, "several souls in your chest" and it is worthwhile to make the energy bound in them available to the Free Self.

All your emotions, thoughts and actions are based on a set of beliefs you created or adopted. Together they form your frame of reference. If you believe that the world is a source of instructive experiences, you can approach people openly and learn from mistakes. This is a meaningful set of beliefs. If you believe that people are out to get you, you will behave anxiously, aggressively or defensively. This is a limiting belief. Success is only possible if it is an option in your frame of reference.

When beliefs are not meaningful, they will limit you. They do not relate to the present: They are either out of touch with Essence, or they ignore the circumstances of the Matrix. These beliefs lead to devaluating, distorting and blocking both yourself and others. They make a meaningful life impossible to reach. Examples include:

- *I am not lovable, not welcome.*
- *I can't make it.*
- *I don't belong, I'm alone, I'm not important.*
- *I'm sick, weak, poor, stupid, lazy, ugly, etc.*

These are examples of limiting beliefs about oneself. They lead to intense negative emotions such as guilt, shame, sadness, and fear. At the beginning of your life it's impossible to grasp the complexity of the reality that is presented to your immature and inexperienced senses. Some people must process traumatic and stressful events without sufficient support. They then mistakenly conclude that some-thing is wrong with them, that they are at fault in some way.

Such limiting beliefs have a long life. They are difficult to influence by conventional means. Argu-ments won't get you anywhere, and good advice is rarely convincing. Anyone who has ever talked with anxious or depressed people knows that most attempts at talking someone out of it are futile.

Logosynthesis has a down-to-earth view on disturbing beliefs. They are energy forms, bound in space and time, in the body or in your personal space. This perspective makes it possible to approach deeply held beliefs as forms of frozen energy—and resolve them. If you retrieve your energy from a negative belief and remove the foreign energy from it, free energy remains. Then you can think again. This does not mean that problems are solved, but you have more resources to find the solution.

Assess and reduce the truth level of limiting beliefs

If you want to weaken a disturbing or limiting belief, the first thing you look for is a short, strong statement that contains the root of the issue, for example:

- *I'm alone.*
- *I'm lazy.*
- *Something is wrong with me.*
- *Everyone is always against me.*

These are the kind of statements that lead people into trouble. You write down the most significant belief on a piece of paper and rate how true you believe it to be on a scale from 0 to 10. 0 means that you don't believe the sentence at all, and 10 means that you are fully convinced. This assessment helps you to calibrate your progress during the exercise.

The following steps help to reduce the truth content of such a disturbing belief—and thus the limitation:

- *Any belief is expressed in language, so you are able to read or hear it. As a first step, you look for the limiting belief in the space around you or in your body. Find written words or a voice saying it to you.*
- *If the belief is written in words, where do you see this text? Find that place: Where is it? How far away is it? How big are the words and in which color and font are they written?*
- *If it is a voice, locate the source of it in the room. Find the voice: What direction is it coming from? How far away is it? What does the voice sound like? Loud or soft? High or low? Do you recognize it?*
- *When you have found out where in the room the belief is located, say the sentences below. Allow enough time between each one for the words to work for you:*

1. *I retrieve all my energy bound up in this belief (state the belief), and I take it to the right place in my Self.*
2. *I remove all non-me energy related to this belief (state the belief), from all of my cells, all of my body and all of my personal space, and I send it to where it truly belongs.*
2. *I retrieve all my energy, bound up in all my reactions to this belief (state the belief), and I take it to the right place in my Self, in the here and now as an adult person.*

- Now look again at the words that you hear and see and assess their level of truth on the scale from 0 to 10. What has changed? Is there another belief hidden behind the first one?

New beliefs can show up after each one you've processed. You can repeat this protocol as often as you like until you are satisfied with the result. Then explore the future after the old beliefs have lost their power.

19.

OTHER PEOPLE STAND IN THE WAY

I love mankind…
It's people I can't stand!
– CHARLES M. SCHULZ

Other people leave energetic traces in your personal space. Some of these traces will stand in the way on your own path. Parents, siblings, teachers, partners, friends or superiors: They all have ideas, wishes and needs that either match or collide with your own. If both sides have similar wishes, differences tend to go unnoticed. When expectations differ, a tension arises in your energy system between your energy and the presence of the other.

When you're working with the perception or image of an important reference person, that representation will always contain energy from that person. This is especially true when your expectations do not match. You can see this in the examples of Cleo and Thomas.

If you want to reduce the influence of others in your life, you can start with any situation that makes you feel uncomfortable—past, present or future. Think about this person X and go through the steps of the Basic Procedure:

- Something is bothering you about this person X. *Decide on a short phrase that accurately describes what it is that bothers you.*
- *Answer the questions:*
  - *How high is the distress you're experiencing on a scale from 0 to 10?*
  - *When you think of this person X, do you have a picture, or do you hear a voice?*
  - *Where do you perceive X in the room when you think of the situation? To the left? On the right? In front of or behind you? Above or below you? How far away?*
- Then say the following sentences:

  1. *I retrieve all my energy bound up in the perception/image of X, and I take it to the right place in my Self.*
  2. *I remove all non-me energy, related to this image of X from all of my cells, all of my body and from all of my personal space, and I send it to where it truly belongs.*
  3. *I retrieve all my energy, bound up in all of my reactions to this image of X, and I take it to the right place in my Self.*

- Let the sentences sink in and work for you, and then examine the result:
    - *How high is the distress now?*
    - *Has the position of X in the room changed?*
    - *Has another perception appeared—related to your past, present, or future?*
    - *If something still bothers you, repeat the procedure starting with the representation that appeared from the previous sequence.*

Ideal people

Ideal people don't exist. Everyone is in constant development until death—and perhaps beyond. This sobering observation does not keep people from wishing for better people—as parents, as partners, as bosses, or as heads of state. Such a wish can be very helpful in some relationships. If parents show their children how to behave well with others, it is easier for them to find their way in the world. If spouses share their wishes and needs and discuss their fulfilment, their relationship can develop and mature.

It becomes problematic when the discrepancy between desire and reality takes on a life of its own. There is no discussion, the reality is not examined, and the wish becomes an independent field. In many partner relationships, there is a secret third person—not of flesh and blood, but one of frozen energy.

This imaginary third person has *all* the qualities that would be attributed to an ideal partner who is capable of the ideal relationship: They are always ready to listen patiently, they are as tender as they are passionate, they read your needs just from looking into your eyes, they do everything for you that you do not like to do for yourself, they always express their affection for you when you want to hear it, they do things together with you in your free time, they are interested in your work, they like your family and your friends, they cook well, are attractive, sexy and monogamous.

Such secret third persons don't exist. And yet, they have ruined many relationships and caused much untold suffering.

A similar dynamic exists between parents and children. 20th-century psychology has discovered that children have needs and that children are better off when these needs are met. Based on this insight, scientists have drawn up a whole catalogue of recommendations that parents should follow in their upbringing and education.

However, in the ivory tower of science and the literature of advice that has emerged from it, it has seldom been acknowledged that these recommendations are unrealistic. Many parents cannot offer their children these conditions. The Matrix simply does not allow this: The resources of time, money and energy are scarce. The stress of work, family and further education overwhelms the parents. Also, parents are not able to give love and attention if they have rarely experienced them as children themselves.

So, ideal parents are rare. No flood of advice and no research findings will change this, on the contrary. Parents who are constantly confronted with the fact that they cannot offer their children what they should, will be extremely susceptible to guilt, shame, fear, and depression. The powerlessness associated with these emotions can turn into anger, rage and wrath at any time.

Logosynthesis for the ideal person

The Basic Procedure of Logosynthesis can easily be applied to people who do not exist. When we dissolve the ideal parents, partners and bosses, real people remain—in the present, not as a memory of the past or as a fantasy in the future.

The sentences of Logosynthesis for ideal people have a special form, as in the example of Myra in chapter 17. I recommend this form of the sentences to those of you who think that other people should live up to your expectations, and also, if you're tired of living with invisible people:

1. *I retrieve all my energy, bound up in this fantasy of an ideal X, and I take it to the right place in my Self.*
2. *I remove all non-me energy, related to this fantasy of an ideal X, from all of my cells, all of my body and from all of my personal space, and I send it to where it truly belongs.*

3. *I retrieve all my energy bound up, in all my reactions to the fact that this ideal X has never existed, doesn't exist and will never exist, and I take it to the right place in my Self.*

20.

YOUR BODY IS
NO MACHINE

Why would nature make a vessel like that,
if not to contain something still more valuable?

– J.K. ROWLING

The body has a special place in people's lives. It is the material carrier of your Self and your task in this world, an instrument that needs to be taken care of—just like a car will get you safely from A to B if it is carefully maintained. Body issues are an important field of application for Logosynthesis. Therefore it is important to understand the place of the body in life.

The body image

Every person has a body image. It provides the brain with information about the body itself, along with its position in the environment. This body image not only serves a biological function: The mind and the Matrix also contribute to it. Much of your identity in this world is based on your body image.

The body is a tool that enables your Self to occupy a place in the world and move around. Some people tend to think of the body as a machine that serves them as they wish. For other people, the body is the business card they show on their entry into the Matrix—to generate or even force respect or admiration. Therefore, the body should be fit, slim, strong, beautiful and sexy.

In the Matrix of the Western world, the body is very important. It should not be sick or show signs of wear and tear. Armies of medics and media are standing by if it doesn't function as desired.

The biggest problems arise when people believe that they *are* their body. If this is the case, a perceived deficiency can quickly become a disability or a deficit of their identity. If something is wrong with your body, something is also wrong with you, the owner of that body.

However, a normal human body will not fulfill all the above needs and desires. Logosynthesis can help you to separate the reality of your body from illusions and wishes that you hold about it.

You can define the state of your body in physical, chemical or biological terms. This definition, in turn, has an effect on your emotions, thoughts, beliefs and behaviors.

Psychological factors increase the intensity of the stress caused by physical symptoms or states, and psychological processes are easier to influence than physical structures. That's why we usually start working on the psychological aspects of a body issue—not with attempts to heal the body. Stress reduction will restore the immune system and speed up healing of physical symptoms.

Disturbances in the flow of energy

With the help of Logosynthesis, you can identify and localize disturbances in your energy system. Memories, fantasies, thoughts and beliefs can freeze energy and lead to suffering. You can resolve the frozen energy patterns with the help of the power of words by using the Logosynthesis Basic Procedure. A few questions to stimulate your thinking:

– Symptoms:
  What signs does the body show?
  Pain, tension, discomfort, agitation
  or fatigue?
– Diagnosis:
  Is there an official diagnosis?
  What is the prognosis?
  What disabilities and disadvantages
  are associated with it?
  What does this mean for the imagined future?
– Treatment:
  How do medications, diets, exercise
  programs, surgery, radiation or
  other treatment modalities effect

the symptoms and your life?
What do you notice during the treatment?
Pain, fatigue, nausea, tension?
- Chronic diseases:
What do you have to give up because of this disease?
What can you do yourself to cope with the situation?
What does your imagined future look like?
- Accidents:
How long will it take to recover?
Will there be permanent damage? What are the consequences of this?
What fantasies do you have about the future?
- Surgery:
What are your ideas about success and failure before the operation?
Will there be scars or pain?
What is no longer possible?

All these areas are connected with perceptions, memories and fantasies, and this means that you can use the Logosynthesis Basic Procedure to reduce the accompanying fear, anxiety, grief, anger and distress. Consequently, you will automatically replace fantasies about what your body could be or should be with facts about how your body is, including illness, disability, injuries, deficits and old age. *C'est la vie*—that's life.

21.

THE FIELDS OF THINGS

**Everything in Nature contains all the powers of Nature.
Everything is made of one hidden stuff.**

– RALPH WALDO EMERSON

Working with the energy fields of matter is a mysterious, even adventurous application of Logosynthesis. From our basic assumptions, however, it is only consistent:

– Everything is energy.
– Energy is either bound or in flow.
– Energy belongs to an object or it doesn't.
– Words move energy.

Again and again, it is shown that material objects leave their energetic traces in the field of people, especially after an injury or an accident. We can completely dissolve these traces with the help of Logosynthesis. How does that work?

The first experience I had with this technique was the neutralization of a scar. In a clumsy moment, I had cut into my left index finger with a large, sharp kitchen knife. After the wound had healed, a disturbing scar remained for years. The site of the cut itself didn't hurt, but the skin around it was tingling—typical for an old scar.

In my experiments with Logosynthesis, I applied the sentences to every aspect of the phenomenon. When I thought about how I could understand and neutralize the scar in the context of the energy model, I came to the following conclusion:

- The energy field of the index finger contains a "memory" of the knife.
- Part of the energy of the knife is frozen in the field of the finger.
- The skin reacts with tingling to the energy pattern of the kitchen knife that is left there.

Based on this logic, I said the first three sentences of Logosynthesis for the representation of the knife in the field of the finger. After the second sentence, something amazing happened: the tingling disappeared. After the third sentence, the skin of the scar was no longer numb.

My adventurous hypothesis that the knife had left energy in my field was confirmed. When I had removed that external energy with the sentences and taken back my own energy, which was bound in reactions to the energy of the knife, the symptom dissolved. The whole procedure took just a few minutes.

Another application of this technique was my work with Joachim. For three years he had had pain in his right leg after colliding with the bumper of a car on a pedestrian crossing. I gave him the following sentences:

1. *I retrieve all my energy bound up in the bumper of this car, and I take it to the right place in my Self.*
2. *I remove all of the energy of this bumper from all my cells, all of my body and from all of my personal space, and I send it to where it truly belongs.*
3. *I retrieve all my energy bound up in all my reactions to this bumper, and I take it to the right place in my Self.*

The pain in Joachim's leg disappeared completely—in seconds. There are many more examples. A Logosynthesis trainee had undergone gynecological surgery ten years ago. Since the operation, she suffered from unbearable abdominal pains every day. I applied the Logosynthesis Basic Procedure to the energy patterns of the surgeon's scalpel and hands. Immediately her whole abdomen started moving inside. The night after the session she suffered severe pains. The next day she was pain free for the first time in years! The energy system of her body had stored energy structures of the surgeon's hands and instruments and had subsequently reacted to this representation, trying to restore the boundaries of her body. This reaction disappeared when the frozen energy patterns were dissolved.

In working with frozen representations of material objects, you find the distressing situation in which these were installed: an attack, an accident, or an operation. Then you identify the moment and place of contact between that material object and the body. Then say the following sentences:

1. *I retrieve all my energy, bound up in the representation of this object X,*
   and I take it to the right place in my Self.
2. *I remove all of the energy of this object X,*
   from all of my cells, all of my body and from all of my personal space,
   and I send it to where it truly belongs.
3. *I retrieve all my energy,*
   bound up in all my reactions to the representation of this object X,
   and I take it to the right place in my Self.

X can be a knife, a bumper or the surgeon's scalpel. It can also be the floor you fell on, a dog bite, a bee sting. If you have correctly identified and located the disturbing energy of the object, it can be quickly neutralized and removed from your field.

22.

THE ENERGY OF THE LAND

**The ache for home
lives in all of us.**

– MAYA ANGELOU

It's not always easy to be where you are. People leave a familiar environment in search of safety, to take up a new job, to get married, or to begin a new life. They long for the variety of the city when they live in the country, or they wish for the peace of the countryside when the city is loud and bustling. When it rains, they want to live in a warm place—until it gets too hot, and they want to cool down.

In every place there is something that is worthwhile and something that challenges you. I live in a wonderful spot at the foot of the Alps. The climate is fine, nature is beautiful, and the place is not overcrowded. However, the motorway is noisy, and you can't enjoy the same cultural program as in a big city. There probably are advantages and disadvantages everywhere, which you can only influence to a limited extent. This applies not only to houses and places but also to climate and continents.

Arrive at home

How can you find peace and quiet, and enjoy where you are? Let us turn again to Logosynthesis. We have already dealt with how to deal with wishes and desires. We'll apply these techniques in simple steps to the geography of a place:

- Concentrate on a place with which you are not satisfied.
- Make some notes about the most important aspects that bother you, such as chaos, noise, traffic jams, concrete, the weather, or the cost of living there.
- Assess the level of distress for the most important aspect on a scale from 0 to 10.
- Focus on a place or situation you desire instead: Are you looking for more variety, more peace, less rain or less noise?
- Create an image or a movie that represents this ideal place.
- Say the following sentences and let each one work until you notice a change:

1. *I retrieve all my energy bound up in the image of this place and in everything it represents, and I take it to the right place in my Self.*
2. *I remove all non-me energy related to this place and everything it represents, from all of my cells,*

all of my body and from all of my personal space, and I send it to where it truly belongs.

3. *I retrieve all my energy bound up in all my reactions to the fact that I am not at the place in this picture, and I take it to the right place in my Self.*

– Now go back to your list of disturbing factors and find out what has changed in your assessment on the scale from 0 to 10.
– Repeat the procedure for other relevant aspects and places.

At first sight, it seems counterintuitive to take your energy back from the desired places. But the problem is that you need this energy at the current place for coping with people and tasks that make your presence here necessary. Even if the present place is not ideal, you had good reasons to choose this station on your life journey.

The secret is to learn to love the place where you are right now, without having to fulfill wishes—it is what it is, and you are here. The application of Logo-synthesis can help you to release the energy that is bound up in other places and to arrive home. Then you will be able to find and enjoy the tranquility or the vitality that you could only have previously dreamt of. When you have arrived in the here and now, all your energy is available for any possible next step that opens up to you. Only then can you judge whether a change of location will serve your mission—or not.

Travel without jet lag

Many travelers suffer from jet lag for days on end. It is said that your physical body travels faster in an airplane than your etheric body. The latter needs more time to arrive at a new place. Some people develop whole procedures to combat jet lag. They go to bed early or skip a night to get their system used to the new place. Others swear by melatonin.

I regularly travel long distances, often with a time difference of six to nine hours. I have experimented with Logosynthesis again and again on these journeys until I found an effective technique to adjust my inner clock to the outer clock. As always, it is based on my understanding of biological and psychological phenomena as energy structures and patterns.

We are energy systems in a space-time field, and this field changes constantly during a long-distance flight. The power of words makes it possible to attune your energy system to the surrounding field. I found a simple sentence to accomplish this:

I attune all my systems to my current location.

This sentence does exactly what it says, and the effect is amazing. The current location has a different time, you have to get used to it. After the working pause of the sentence, your energy system immediately adapts to the time of day of the new place, and your awareness changes accordingly. Whereas in the past, after a long flight, I didn't know where my head was, I now arrive at the local time, not only according to the clock, but also in my own sense of time.

When I fly westwards and am awake, I repeat the above jetlag sentence every two hours and let it work. Then I always feel a small shift of the inner clock, and I keep the sense of time, which would normally get lost during a flight.

With the help of this sentence, I can take off at noon in Zurich and land in New York or Montreal without a trace of jet lag. When I get there, it's 4:00 p.m., and it feels that way. Because I rested on the plane, I am relaxed. So, it's alright if the day lasts a long time.

It's different going east. Then, I must give up the time I gained heading west. Because I mainly sleep on the way, I say the sentence on arrival and afterwards a few more times before I reach my final destination. Once there, I lie down to rest. I sleep as long as I feel like it. I do not need any other techniques, and I go with the flow. Usually I am rested the next morning, without feeling tired of traveling.

Travel trance

There are many reasons to be annoyed during a journey: waiting at airports, noisy or crowded seating with neighbors, cheap perfumes, bad food or seats that are not to your liking. To reduce irritation when travelling, I have developed a technique I call

141

my *travel trance*. This is a state of quiet relaxation that enables me to travel in a relaxed way at any time. Because I have practiced it many times, I can put my body and my mind into the travel trance quickly and easily.

If you are not yet familiar with this exercise, you can induce this trance by applying Logosynthesis. This is possible, whether the journey by car, train or plane has already begun, or you are standing in a queue—at the check-in, baggage claim or immigration desk.

The technique consists of speaking the Logosynthesis sentences for everything you perceive—what you see, hear, feel, smell and taste. Open your senses and say a sequence of the sentences for the first thing that strikes you. On a train, for example, this might be the lights, your neighbor's face, the sound of the wheels on the tracks, the voice from the loudspeaker at the station, the cushion of your seat in your back, the smell of the brakes or the taste of the coffee you just drank. While you concentrate on the perception, you say the sentences in the usual way:

1. *I retrieve all my energy bound up in this perception X,*
   and I take it to the right place in my Self.
2. *I remove all non-me energy related to this perception X,*
   from all of my cells, all of my body and from all of

my personal space, and I send it to where it truly belongs.

3. *I retrieve all my energy, bound up in all my reactions to this perception X,*
    and I take it to the right place in my Self.

It is not important if your perception is immediately associated with distress or discomfort. You say the sentences for one aspect of the environment, let them sink in, and let that aspect fade away. Then focus on the next thing that comes into your mind. You will notice that after several times of repeating the sentences, you will achieve a pleasant state of relaxation. You won't care about the length of the queue at customs, or the fact that you must take off your shoes or open your carry-on luggage again.

Have a great trip!

23.

THE FIELDS OF
THE MATRIX

It is not the consciousness of men that determines
their being, but, on the contrary, their social being
that determines their consciousness.

– KARL MARX

The energy field of the world, the Matrix, contains social, economic, organizational, political, cultural, national and continental energy patterns: *socio-energetic fields*. Whoever enters this world, slowly learns about these patterns through education and training. Parents and school teach and model the patterns and the child absorbs them unconsciously. The Matrix is to you what water is to fish: life without it is unimaginable.

Nowadays, people often think that their parents determine or have determined their life. If you take a closer look, you'll see that they have taken their basic attitude, their purpose in life and their forms of communication from society. They could not exert great influence on their living conditions. My own parents' way of life was very much determined by three factors: their farming village, their strong faith, and the optimism of society after the Second World War. They shared this basic attitude with many others at that time, and they would hardly have thought of deviating from it.

The Matrix defines what and how you can and should think. You tend to absorb the frequencies of the socio-energetic fields of the Matrix that you are part of and that you resonate with. If at all, people slowly become aware of its full influence—including its resources and limitations.

Society gives everyone a script to create their own life, like in a movie or novel. Children need fairy tales, and adults need stories to develop their understanding of the world.

Consciousness of the Matrix is as important as consciousness of your Essence, because your life takes place in the Matrix. That is where your life mission must be accomplished. From our understanding of human beings, your Essence has chosen exactly these socio-energetic fields as a playground, school, laboratory, or stage, to fulfil your mission.

Every aspect of the Matrix is a learning field for your Essence: family, gender, ethnicity, class, religion, status, politics, age, prosperity, nationality, language or the culture in its entirety. People deal with these fields of learning in different ways. The existence of the Self at the interface between Essence and the Matrix presents people with both enormous challenges and great opportunities. There are three general patterns:

1. The Self's connection with Essence is lost.
2. The Self is not able to connect to the Matrix and its resources.
3. Dynamic interaction of the Self with Essence and the Matrix—in the service of your mission.

These patterns are not carved in stone, but often people are leaning in one direction or another. Healing and development allow you to move more and more freely between these two poles of your existence. How does your energy flow between your Essence and the Matrix?

1. Focus Matrix: Connection to Essence is lost

In this pattern, your contact with the Matrix is so overwhelming that the consciousness of your Essence is pushed to the background. In this case, the Matrix becomes your only reality. Consequently, your state of being depends on whether your material, physical and psychological needs are met. If this is the case, you will be able to live a peaceful life.

If your needs are not met, you'll be in trouble. The energy that's stored in your memories, beliefs and convictions limits your consciousness and your potential. Depending on the signals that reach you from the Matrix, you feel ashamed, guilty, passive, sad, fearful or angry. The fulfillment of your mission moves further and further out of reach.

2. Focus Essence: Essence is not able to access the Matrix and its potential

The second pattern is hardly more constructive. You are aware that you come from Essence, and that you have a purpose in this life—but no one is interested. You are aware of your task, but you seem to be the only person who takes it seriously. You run into an invisible wall whenever you want to put something into practice.

It is difficult for you to understand what exactly is going on, and you cannot access the resources you need to accomplish your task. You lack connections, financial resources, education, training, or social status to be recognized in your mission.

3. The dynamic interaction between Essence and the Matrix

In the third position, your Free Self is able to switch easily between the potential of your Essence and the resources of the Matrix. This position makes it possible for your Free Self to enter the Matrix from the awareness of your Essence and to engage itself there. Your energy flows freely, you are aware of your mission and you can occupy the intersections in your environment that you need to in order to fulfill your tasks. You acquire the right education, get to know the right people, build a network of like-minded people and find time and opportunities to implement your calling in a profession.

The first two positions lead to tension. In the third, you can tap into the resources of the Matrix and use them in the service of your mission. How do you do that? Below, I have listed the most important questions for human development:

- *Why are you in this world?*
- *Why did you choose this environment, this Matrix, for this mission?*
- *When, how and where do you experience the Matrix as disturbing your path?*
- *When, how and where do you experience the Matrix as supporting your path?*

People often think that the Matrix blocks the fulfillment of their mission because their energy is tied up in experiences of lack and failure. They deduce that there is something wrong with either themselves or their environment—or even both. This prevents them from recognizing the potential of the Matrix and using it to their advantage.

The Matrix can also support you in your task in life. Once you know what you are here for and recognize how important the Matrix is for the fulfillment of this mission, it will provide resources for you where and whenever it can. The Scottish mountaineer and author William Hutchison Murray put it this way:

Until you commit, there is hesitation, the chance to retreat. The moment you commit, providence moves too. All kinds of things happen to help you, which would never have happened otherwise.

If you are serious in your commitment, the whole world will commit to fulfilling your mission.

Logosynthesis in the Matrix

When you are aware of both the mission of your Essence and the resources of the Matrix, you can use Logosynthesis to free your energy for your task. For this purpose, I will give you an example from my own story:

Before I discovered Logosynthesis, I could hardly believe that guided change was easy. I had worked with many of the existing models. I had searched for a long time for resources and methods for my clients and I felt exhausted, dissatisfied and alone.

Then, in the course of 2005, when I realized that I could use the creative energy of words effectively and efficiently, I found that hardly anyone in my environment understood me.

Guiding people in overcoming fear, guilt, grief and trauma has always been challenging; and spirituality has barely played a role in conventional therapeutic wisdom. In the prevailing schools, nothing could adequately explain what happened in my sessions.

In the beginning, I looked for explanations using existing models but did not find any. Phenomena such as hypnosis, the placebo effect or affirmations did not offer any new insights—in contrast, they seemed to rationalize or disguise the phenomenon of the power of words. It was only when I developed an energy framework that the power of Logosynthesis became clear to me to its full extent:

- Essence is a form of energy that shapes and gives meaning to our lives.
- Words and sentences can focus this energy—in the service of healing and development.

The combination of the creative potential of Essence with the power of words finally convinced me. Not only that, but I also found receptors in the Matrix: Other people had similar questions and wanted to learn from me and with me. Thus, a flourishing, growing community emerged that asked new questions and began finding new answers. The last question of this book is for you:

How can you use the energy of the Matrix for the mission of your Essence?

24.

TIPS AND TRICKS

Life is a lively process of becoming.

– DOUGLAS MACARTHUR

The application of the Logosynthesis sentences looks very simple at first sight. In practice, it is less easy. My other books on Logosynthesis will teach you many more ways to approach different issues. This chapter offers some practical tips to overcome every-day issues in the application of the Basic Procedure:

- drinking water
- salami and artichokes
- the limits of self-application
- the notes, the chords and the music

Drink water

Often people feel weak, tired, confused, a little nauseous or dizzy after speaking a sentence—often after the first or second sentence but rarely after the third. These symptoms are normal responses to the release of bound energy. When your energy begins to flow again, the information in the cells is rearranged.

You do not need to pay special attention to these symptoms. In most cases, they tend to disappear spontaneously when the person drinks water. Therefore, always have a jug or bottle of fresh water ready when you work with the sentences.

Salami and artichokes

Many people who begin to use Logosynthesis are amazed at what is possible in a short time. They sometimes become bold and wonder if they can release all their energy, which is bound up in the past, present and future, in a single pass. That sounds logical—and it would be very nice! However, in most situations you need to make small steps in the Logosynthesis Basic Procedure—slice by slice, like when you're eating salami. Your body and your mind need time to process the changes induced by the resolution of frozen energy. In the past, your system was flooded by new information you weren't able to process, and that was when your energy was frozen into patterns. The steps in the healing and development process need to allow for restoration and to avoid a repetition of such flooding.

That is why we examine the individual aspects of perceptions and reactions in detail. The more precisely steps are defined, the easier we can observe any progress. Steps that are too large will often confirm disturbing patterns, whereas every successful step, however small, encourages us to go further and deeper in the process. It is like eating artichokes: You advance to the heart, layer by layer.

The limits of self-application

If you are working with Logosynthesis on your own, it is important to allow enough time to read this book, and other ones, to make sure that you understand the principles and practice properly. This creates the possibility for pleasant surprises and reduces the risk of you being disappointed.

However, you cannot pull yourself out of the swamp by your own hair, not even with Logosynthesis. Many everyday problems can be tackled and solved with the help of the Basic Procedure, but there are also situations in which you will not get ahead on your own. It is important to recognize these.

Often these are issues related to early experiences of loneliness, grief, guilt, and trauma. From these experiences, people come to the conclusion that they are alone and thus have to do everything alone. Later in life they are not able to recognize that help and support could come from outside.

If you think that you are alone and must find a way out of suffering on your own, then you have a limiting belief that excludes help from others. In that case, I recommend you say the sentences of Logosynthesis for the belief: "No one can help me." Then the chance increases that you can trust a professional as a companion on your path from survival to fulfilment.

The notes, the chords and the music

For many people, the Logosynthesis sentences take some getting used to. They look for an explanation that fits into their familiar frame of reference, or they even refuse to use the methods. It is a challenge to accept a model in which the basic assumptions sound very simple but go far beyond traditional models of guided change.

In our books and seminars for professionals, we explain the theory and dynamics of the energy model of Logosynthesis from many different angles. However, to make the sentences work for your issues, you do not need to understand their meaning, nor the mechanism behind them. It is enough to listen to the person who offers them and to repeat each sentence as spoken.

Logosynthesis does not work miracles, even if it often feels like it. The so-called miracles that are experienced in Logosynthesis are based on a carefully tested, coherent system. This system has principles, concepts based on these principles, and precisely applied methods.

Especially in the beginning, many people tend to change the techniques of Logosynthesis even before they have understood its philosophical and theoretical basis at a deeper level. They add elements without realizing that there is a reason for the apparent simplicity of the methods. Or they try to deal with many subjects at once, rather than in slices as in the salami principle.

Some people even try to add or create "positive" alternatives without realizing that our Essence is the universal resource—in every single case. The power of the words in the Logosynthesis sentences activates Essence immediately, without the interference of the conscious, rational mind.

I am aware that the seemingly simple structure of the methods of Logosynthesis can invite people to change or "improve" them. However, I strongly recommend that you let the sentences work as described in our books and training. Each word, each element, has been carefully tested and has proven to be effective many times.

When you learn to play a musical instrument, you must practice for a long time before real music can be heard from the individual notes and chords. In this book, you will find the notes and some chords of Logosynthesis. The music comes with experience, practice, reading and training.

25.

CONCLUSION

There is no real ending...

– FRANK HERBERT

This little book contains a wealth of information about Logosynthesis. This will be enough for the application to smaller issues in everyday life. However, the model offers more. It is a comprehensive system for healing and development—social, personal and spiritual.

If you delve deeper into Logosynthesis, you will understand signals and symptoms better. With increasing understanding, you can apply the methods described here and elsewhere, with greater skill and precision.

The Logosynthesis Basic Procedure presented in this book is only one method from a whole range of options for self-coaching and for the professional support of people in their process of healing and development. The same applies to the terms presented: These help to understand human emotions, thoughts and behavior patterns as energy patterns and to improve either your own situation, or that of your clients in practice.

There are several options for understanding and applying Logosynthesis at a deeper level:

- My book *Self Coaching with Logosynthesis®. How the Power of Words Can Change Your Life.* offers a significant deepening of this process. It contains many examples from my practice and describes additional techniques.
- Specialists from the teaching and helping professions will find a detailed description of the theory, the Basic Procedure and concrete case studies in my book: *Logosynthesis®. Healing with words. A Handbook for the Helping Professions* with a Preface by Dr. Fred Gallo.
- The YouTube channel *The Origin of Logosynthesis®* shows excerpts from sessions with real clients in several languages—at the level presented in this book. The videos give examples of the professional application of Logosynthesis to different personal issues. In the login area of the website of LIA, the Logosynthesis International Association, longer videos show the resolution of deep-rooted sources of trauma and fear.
- On Facebook you can find groups at different levels of experience and in different languages. The most important Facebook groups in English are *Logosynthesis* for a general audience and *Logosynthesis Trainees E* for people in training. These groups help you to find answers to many

questions about the model and its areas of application.

- There are also Logosynthesis groups in several languages on LinkedIn.
- Certified instructors offer open courses in the field of Logosynthesis. Issues include self-coaching and how to deal with money, time, stress or procrastination. In these courses, you learn to recognize blocks and to dissolve them yourself with the help of Logosynthesis.
- The most instructive way to learn Logosynthesis is to work on your issues with the help of an experienced professional. Often people stop using it when painful issues come to the surface, because it is tedious to process them alone. Only a few sessions will help you to overcome blocks and to manage the subsequent steps on your own. Such support is both possible and effective online. On the LIA website you will find a list of experts.
- If you are trained as a professional in psychotherapy, counseling, coaching or education, you can attend advanced training to become a Practitioner and Master Practitioner of the Logosynthesis International Association. In these courses, we teach a wide range of subjects on the theory, attitude, methods and skills related to the application of Logosynthesis in the practice of the participants.

You can find more details in the appendix.

APPENDIX

This appendix contains additional information on various themes:

- author portrait
- disclaimer
- Logosynthesis books
- Logosynthesis on the Internet
- learning Logosynthesis
- the Logosynthesis Basic Procedure in a nutshell

26.

ABOUT THE AUTHOR

After my studies in social and clinical psychology I started my professional life as an assistant professor at the Medical Faculty of the Free University of Amsterdam in the Netherlands. There, I gained firsthand experience as a scientist and trainer. After a few years I discovered my preference for therapeutic work over an academic career and took a position in the treatment of patients and the management of a high-altitude clinic in Davos, Switzerland. Later, becoming self-employed, I founded an institute for professional training in coaching, counseling and organizational development in Switzerland and managed this for many years.

Since the beginning of my professional development, I have worked intensively in many therapeutic approaches. I trained in bioenergetics, gestalt therapy, transactional analysis, hypnotherapy, NLP, EMDR, and energy psychology. In 2005, I discovered the principles of Logosynthesis. Since then, I've been continually developing this model.

I founded the Institute for Logosynthesis® in Bad Ragaz (CH) and handed it over to my successor, Dr. med. Suzanne von Blumenthal, in 2017.

In my long professional career I have written and published books in several languages—along with shorter articles and essays. I have a practice for coaching and psychotherapy in Switzerland, and I like to travel and teach Logosynthesis worldwide.

27.

DISCLAIMER

The information contained in this book is educational in nature and is provided only as general information. Logosynthesis is a relatively new approach and the extent of its effectiveness, as well as its risks and benefits are not fully known. The reader agrees to assume and accept full responsibility for any and all risks associated with reading this book and using Logosynthesis as a result. The reader understands that if he or she chooses to use Logosynthesis, emotional or physical sensations or additional unresolved memories may surface which could be perceived as negative side effects. Emotional material may continue to surface after using Logosynthesis, indicating that other issues may need to be addressed. Previously vivid or traumatic memories may fade which could adversely impact your ability to provide detailed legal testimony regarding a traumatic incident.

The information presented in this text is not intended to represent that Logosynthesis is used to diagnose, treat, cure, or prevent any disease or psychological disorder. Logosynthesis is not a substitute for medical or psychological treatment. The case reports and information presented in this text do not constitute a warranty, guarantee, or prediction regarding the outcome of an individual using Logosynthesis for any particular issue. The author makes no warranty, guarantee, or prediction regarding any outcome for using Logosynthesis for any particular issue. The information presented in this book is intended only for your own personal use.

In order to use Logosynthesis with others, you need to become sufficiently trained and qualified as a Practitioner in Logosynthesis®. While all materials and links to other resources are posted in good faith, the accuracy, validity, effectiveness, completeness, or usefulness of any information herein, as with any publication, cannot be guaranteed. The author accepts no responsibility or liability whatsoever for the use or misuse of the information contained in this book. Please seek professional advice as appropriate before implementing any protocol or opinion expressed in this book, and before making any health decisions. If any court of law rules that any part of the Disclaimer is invalid, the Disclaimer stands as if those parts were struck out. By continuing to read this text you agree to all of the above.

28.

LOGOSYNTHESIS
BOOKS

1. The book for self-application

Willem Lammers (2015). Self-Coaching with Logosynthesis: How the Power of Words Can Change Your Life. Bad Ragaz, Switzerland: The Origin of Logosynthesis®.

The book is easy to read and contains powerful exercises to solve everyday problems. It also contains fascinating, real-life examples of Logosynthesis in action. You will learn how to move beyond disturbing memories, frightening fantasies and limiting beliefs, and finally take control of your own life—so that the suffering stops. This book is also published in German, Italian and Serbian.

2. The book for professionals

Willem Lammers (2015). *Logosynthesis. Healing with Words. A Handbook for the Helping Professions with a Preface by Dr. Fred Gallo.* Bad Ragaz, Switzerland: The Origin of Logosynthesis®.

This practical book offers an introduction to Logosynthesis for professionals in coaching, counseling and psychotherapy. It describes the philosophy, the model and important methods of Logosynthesis, with many examples and verbatim protocols of actual sessions with clients. According to the model of Logosynthesis, unpleasant experiences, stressful memories with their corresponding frozen reactions are stored in our energy field. Similar events, situations or people reactivate these limiting patterns automatically, creating difficulties. This book is also available in German and Dutch.

3. Examples from daily practice

Willem Lammers (2019). *Minute Miracles: The Practice of Logosynthesis®.* (Logosynthesis Live series, Vol. 1). Bad Ragaz, Switzerland: The Origin of Logosynthesis®.

This book contains many impressive examples of the effects of Logosynthesis®, a new model for self-coaching and for accompanying people during the process of change and development. In his earlier books, Willem Lammers described Logosynthesis for professional work and as a model for self-coaching. This book shares descriptions of actual sessions with real clients. He demonstrates the possibilities and potential of Logosynthesis in everyday practice. This book is also available in German, Dutch and Italian.

4. Logosynthesis and emotions

Willem Lammers (2020). *Reclaiming Your Energy from Your Emotions: States of the Mind in*

Logosynthesis®. (Logosynthesis Live series, Vol. 2). Bad Ragaz, Switzerland: The Origin of Logosynthesis®.

Emotions don't exist in an empty space; they are reaction patterns to the perception of the world around us. If that perception is clear, our reactions will be adequate, but perceptions can also be distorted by memories of a painful past, the imagination of a threatening future, or rigid beliefs that limit us in living our mission on this earth. Logosynthesis supports people to let go of frozen patterns in their emotions.

5. Logosynthesis and the spiritual dimension

Willem Lammers (2020). *Sparks at Dawn: Awakening with Logosynthesis®. Reflections on the Journey.* (Logosynthesis Live series, Vol. 3). Bad Ragaz, Switzerland: The Origin of Logosynthesis®.

This book is a collection of essays on human experience, on ordinary and extraordinary aspects of living, from a spiritual perspective. Each lesson, written at dawn and inspired by the liminal state between asleep and awake, reveals how the Matrix of human expectations interface with the universal flow from your Essence.

Other publications

More and more people are writing about their work with Logosynthesis. You can find a complete list of all publications about Logosynthesis can be found on the website of the Logosynthesis International Association: www.logosynthesis.international.

29.

LOGOSYNTHESIS ON THE INTERNET

Logosynthesis International Association (LIA)

www.logosynthesis.international

LIA, the Logosynthesis International Association, supports the development and spreading of Logosynthesis in the world via a number of activities: maintaining international and local websites, by managing a directory of certified professionals and by developing training standards for those who wish to learn how to use Logosynthesis in their profession as coaches, consultants or psychotherapists.

On the LIA website, you can find up-to-date information on Logosynthesis training and providers of seminars for self-coaching, and for the training and certification of professionals. The website also contains a list of trained and certified specialists in Logosynthesis, who can support you professionally, either directly or online.

Willem Lammers—The Origin of Logosynthesis®

www.logosynthesis.net

On this website of the author, Dr. Willem Lammers, you will find up-to-date information about Logosynthesis. You can also subscribe to his newsletter: *Sparks. The Latest from Logosynthesis®*. You will receive regular information with video links, application examples, seminars and other issues related to Logosynthesis.

Facebook and LinkedIn

There are many groups on Facebook and LinkedIn in several languages related to the personal and professional use of Logosynthesis. Search for: Logosynthesis, Logosynthese, Logosynthèse, Logosintesi and Logosynthese Nederlands.

YouTube

Dr. Willem Lammers' channel on YouTube is called *The Origin of Logosynthesis®*. It contains a series of videos in different languages in which Logosynthesis is applied with clients and in relation to specific issues. The QR code below opens the link.

30.

LEARNING LOGOSYNTHESIS

Learning for yourself

If you want to use Logosynthesis for your own personal and spiritual development, there are the following possibilities (as of 2020):

- Various books on self-application
- Open groups on Facebook and LinkedIn
- Introduction workshops in Logosynthesis as self-application
- Thematic workshops that focus on the application of Logosynthesis in a specific field, such as love, work, health or wealth
- Workshops lasting several days for dealing with deeper personal issues.

You can find the dates and further details on the LIA website: www.Logosynthesis.international.

Advanced Training in Logosynthesis for Professionals

The principles of Logosynthesis can be learned either in a few days in person, or online over several weeks, by trained professionals in the fields of coaching, counseling and psychotherapy. The seminar Logosynthesis Basic teaches the philosophy, the model, the principles behind the method and the Basic Procedure. You learn to use the methods for yourself and others. The seminars are open to professionals and trainees in the helping and teaching professions.

For trained professionals in coaching, counseling, psychotherapy and education there is a training program for Practitioners in Logosynthesis®. It consists of the following elements:

- Logosynthesis Basic
- seminars for personal development
- theme seminars
- practice groups
- supervision
- a written paper

This training is certified by LIA, the Logosynthesis International Association. You can find further details about training on the website of the association: www.logosynthesis.international.

31.

THE BASIC PROCEDURE IN A NUTSHELL

Here's a summary of the Logosynthesis Basic Procedure:

–   Find a quiet place where you can practice undisturbed.
–   Find an issue in which you want to experience the increased influence of your Essence.
–   Choose an aspect X from this issue that disturbs or distresses you: a memory, a fantasy or a limiting belief that is connected with unpleasant emotions, physical sensations or thoughts.
–   Examine where you perceive X in your body or your personal space. What do you see, hear or sense?
–   Find the level of distress you're experiencing—on a scale from 0 (no distress) to 10 (extreme distress).
–   Say the first sentence of the sequence:

*I retrieve all my energy bound up in X
(perception, thought, event, person, place)*

and I take it to the right place in my Self.

- Let the sentence work for a few minutes and explore the effect on your perceptions, your body, on your thinking, and your emotions.
- Say the second sentence:

I remove all non-me energy related to X (perception, thought, event, person, place), from all of my cells, all of my body and from all of my personal space, and I send it to where it truly belongs.

- Let the sentence work for a few minutes and explore the effect on your perceptions, your body, on your thinking and your emotions.
- Then say the third sentence in the sequence:

I retrieve all my energy, bound up in all my reactions to X (perception, thought, event, person, place), and I take it to the right place in my Self.

- Examine the changes in your body and in your personal space.
- Examine the level of distress you feel about X again reassess the score on the scale from 0 to 10.
- Have a glass of water.
- Imagine your future and examine whether and how the issue emerges.
- If so, treat the next aspect in a new sequence.

- If everything is resolved and your rating is between a 0 and a 3, say the fourth sentence:

I attune all my systems to this new awareness.

- Now imagine a future in which the issue is no longer a problem: What will you do instead?

Download Worksheet
With the help of this QR code you can download a worksheet for your application of the Logosynthesis Basic Procedure.

P.S.

WILL YOU HELP US?

Did you enjoy this book? If so, please take ten minutes and publish a short review on your favorite social media channel. In this way, you help us to spread and share Logosynthesis and you support other people on their path of healing and development. Once you've done this, then please send a copy of your review to info@logosynthesis.net, and I will thank you personally.

Thanks very much in advance, and I'm looking forward to your comments!

Dr. Willem Lammers.

Made in United States
Troutdale, OR
08/19/2024

22141082R00106